]

Winner of the Jeanne Clarke Local History Award.

Longlisted for the 2022/2023 First Nations Communities Read Award.

Nominated for the Rocky Mountain Book Award, Alberta's children's choice award.

"A powerful novel based on the true story of Proverbs's biological mother and aunt."

**GLOBE & MAIL**

"In *Aggie & Mudgy*, Wendy Proverbs skillfully weaves a story that invites young readers to engage in a learning experience articulated within a structure reflective of traditional storytelling. Proverbs's story not only provides insight into the reality of the removal of children to residential schools, but also gives insights and examples of Kaska Dena culture and traditions. These characters will stay with young readers and inspire them to embark on further learning."

**MICHELLE GOOD** award-winning author of *Five Little Indians*

"*Aggie & Mudgy* is a beautiful book. This story captures the warmth of a family, then the heartbreak of a family, and finally comes full circle to the love in a family. The new sights and experiences on their journey keep one interested. The ending made me cry in a good way. I highly recommend this book."

BEV SELLARS author of *They Called Me Number One: Secrets and Survival at an Indian Residential School*

"An important recounting of the Kaska Dena experience where children were removed from their families and taken impossibly great distances to residential schools. *Aggie & Mudgy* highlights how imperative it was for even the very young, such as these two Kaska Dena girls, to become their own heroes. An example of the enduring legacy of intergenerational memory and of honouring and keeping the stories of these children alive."

CHRISTY JORDAN-FENTON co-author of *Fatty Legs: A True Story*

"An important recounting of the Kaska Dena experience where children were removed from their families and taken impossibly great distances to residential schools. *Aggie & Mudgy* highlights how imperative it was for even the very young, such as these two Kaska Dena girls, to become their own heroes. An example of the enduring legacy of intergenerational memory and of honouring and keeping the stories of these children alive."

**CHRISTY JORDAN-FENTON** co-author of *Fatty Legs: A True Story*

"*Aggie & Mudgy* is an exceptional middle grade novel that shines with warmth, knowledge & honesty."

**THUNDERBIRD WOMAN READS**

"This title definitely helps to fill in the gaps for all Canadians about the history of residential schools, and the many miles away from their own families and communities that some children were forced to travel to get there. It is also a powerful demonstration to the importance of connecting (or reconnecting) to kin, community and culture."

**CANADIAN CHILDREN'S BOOK NEWS** Winter 2021

# AGGIE & MUDGY

## The Journey of Two Kaska Dena Children

### WENDY PROVERBS
ILLUSTRATIONS BY ALYSSA KOSKI

WANDERING FOX  An imprint of
HERITAGE HOUSE PUBLISHING

Wandering Fox Books
An imprint of Heritage House Publishing Company Ltd.
heritagehouse.ca

*Cataloguing information available from*
*Library and Archives Canada*
978-1-77203-375-5 (paperback)
978-1-77203-376-2 (e-book)

Cover and interior illustrations by Alyssa Koski
Map by Eric Leinberger
Cover and interior book design by Setareh Ashrafologhalai
The interior of this book was produced on 100% post-con-
sumer paper, processed chlorine-free and printed with
vegetable-based inks.

Heritage House gratefully acknowledges that the land on
which we live and work is within the traditional territo-
ries of the Lkwungen (Esquimalt and Songhees), Malahat,
Pacheedaht, Scia'new, T'Sou-ke, and W̱SÁNEĆ (Pauquachin,
Tsartlip, Tsawout, Tseycum) Peoples.

We acknowledge the financial support of the Government of
Canada through the Canada Book Fund (CBF) and the Canada
Council for the Arts, and the Province of British Columbia
through the British Columbia Arts Council and the Book
Publishing Tax Credit.

26 25 24 23 22    2 3 4 5 6

Printed in Canada

*To all the children*
*finding their way home.*

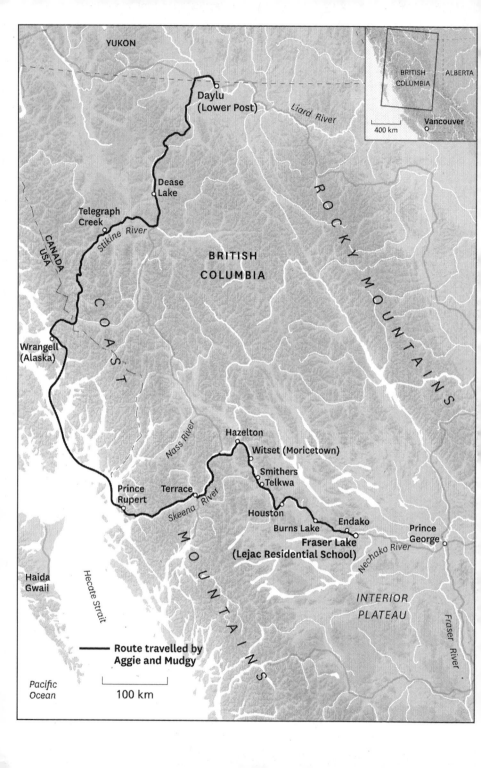

# Author's Note

THIS IS a story of two young Kaska Dena girls' journey from their homeland on the BC-Yukon border, to the steps of Lejac Residential School, in central BC, in the 1920s. It is based on my aunt's memoir depicting the journey she took with my birth mother. The story unfolds in contemporary times told by a fictionalized grandmother, Nan, to her eight-year-old granddaughter, Maddy.

In keeping with the oral tradition of her ancestors, Nan teaches her granddaughter about her past by way of story. It slowly unfolds over several days as Nan and Maddy go about their daily routines. This is my way of telling my personal history to a fictional granddaughter living in today's world.

As Maddy listens to Nan tell her about the girls' journey, she learns how it changed their lives forever, and her young mind asks questions that any child might ask. For example, Maddy wonders why they had to change their Kaska names to anglicized names, providing Nan an opportunity to teach her granddaughter about this dark aspect of her ancestors' past. The story offers a glimpse into the impacts of colonization at a level Maddy can begin to understand. It also provides a lovely example of how the sisters fashioned their anglicized names into ones that they could own and like. Renamed by the church as Agnes and Martha, the girls decided to call themselves Aggie and Mudgy.

The story Nan tells Maddy is not, however, about what Aggie and Mudgy experience at residential school. It focuses instead on the expedition that takes them from their home in Daylu (Lower Post), near the BC–Yukon border, to Lejac Residential School on the shores of Fraser Lake in central BC. The girls, aged eight and six, travel approximately 1,600 kilometres by riverboat, truck, paddlewheeler, steamship, and train—an exceptionally long journey even by today's standards, let alone for two young girls who had never been outside their remote village.

A priest wearing a long black robe accompanies them, an unkind man who physically abuses them when they don't do as they're told. At one point, they try to escape but are unsuccessful. The story of the journey ends just as the huge residential school doors bang shut behind the girls.

To my knowledge, the literature published about Indigenous children's travels from their home communities to the schools is not extensive. My mother and aunt's residential school experiences were like those of their peers—comprised of well-documented injustices, now widely acknowledged as a national shame.

Exposed to daily Christian indoctrination, they were punished and deprived of their culture, language, and families. This has been recognized as a form of cultural genocide by former Supreme Court justice Beverley McLachlin. Thankfully, these heartbreaking stories are coming to light more and more often, educating people about the tragic consequences and intergenerational trauma that continues today.

My story offers a slightly different way into learning about this past by detailing the exceptional journey of my aunt and birth mother during a time when travel was an arduous undertaking. It also offers a glimpse into the transitional period of post-European contact, when small towns emerged and grew as a result of booming resource development.

MY AUNT'S memoir planted the seeds of this story long ago. Writing Aggie and Mudgy's story has drawn me closer to my ancestral roots. Like thousands of other Indigenous children in Canada, I'm part of this story. I was an infant during the sweeping scoop of Indigenous children taken from their home communities and placed with non-Indigenous families.

I was a young adult when I began to search for my birth family. My search led me to some siblings, but I was too late to meet Mudgy, my birth mother. She had passed away several years earlier. Had my mother and aunt lived out their lives in the small northern community where they were born, who knows where life might have led them and me?

Weaving my story through this fictionalized narrative enables me to share my ancestors' historic journey, thereby offering readers insight into what it might have been like for young children to travel so incredibly far from their homeland and loved ones so long ago. My goal is to help younger generations, both Indigenous and non-Indigenous, learn more about our country's past. By learning about where we came from, we can begin to see how these stories shape who we are today.

## CHAPTER ONE
# Rupert Lane

A MATURE woman waits silently. Her dark hair is peppered with silver streaks and tied back in a ponytail. Her brown eyes twinkle with mischief. She eases herself onto a plush, dusty rose-coloured loveseat and delights in the comforting glow of the late afternoon sunshine.

Off to the side of the room, near a large bay window, is a round wooden table with a nest of four chairs, each covered in pastel suede. In the centre of the table, a large turquoise tea towel covers an easel. Underneath, a canvas painting rests alone on the table.

Inhaling deeply, the woman whispers to herself, "Remember, it is the process and not the final outcome that's critical to all emerging artists. The process."

Low murmurs seep from under the tea towel: "Set me free... Uncover me... It is time..." The draping jerks amid a mournful "Set meeee freeeeeee..." Then the whispering morphs into a high pitch, and the tea towel moves erratically: "UNCOVER MEEEEEEEEE..."

"All right, Maddy. Let's uncover your masterpiece now. Please use your inside voice," the woman says with a mock-stern face.

"Yeaaaaah, thank you, Nan." Eight-year-old Maddy grins as she emerges from under the table, where the easel stands. "You're gonna love my painting. It is one of my best ones yet, and I need you to like it times one hundred, 'cause I wanna give it to Mommy for Christmas. You need to look at it *very* closely."

Maddy started calling her grandmother *Nan* a long time ago. It was just so much more work to say "grandma" or "grandmother" all the time, and despite her creativity, Maddy is a practical girl in many ways. Her Nan looks down at her and tenderly cups her small face in her fine brown hands.

"Hear ye! Hear ye!" Nan gleefully announces. "To all in this house, the unveiling will now commence of Miss Maddy's latest work of art. Come forth and witness this great occasion!"

Maddy beams and then cocks her ear. She hears a *click, click, click* on the floor. It's Buskers, her rescue dog, coming to see what the fuss is all about. Buskers is not the most handsome of animals; his pedigree is questionable, and his stature is squat. He has one lopsided ear that shoots straight up when he spots potential prey, especially squirrels with twitchy tails.

With Buskers by her side, Nan turns to Maddy and says, "Miss Maddy, please do us the honour and unveil your latest work of art for all to witness."

"Why, *thank you*, Nan and Buskers," says Maddy, mimicking the dignified tone she's often heard artists use at Nan's gallery openings. "I am really, really happy to be here to share my latest painting. Here it is. TA-DA!" With a flourish, Maddy pulls the tea towel off of her painting.

Nan examines it closely. After all, she is an experienced art critic and gallery owner, who specializes in discovering new artists. Nan is almost as passionate about her gallery as she is about Maddy.

The painting looks small on the easel, but it shines with a rainbow of vibrant colours and pleasing composition. It's similar to the folk art of a Maud Lewis painting—simple but striking. Purple and yellow dominate much of the space. Buskers is in the foreground with a family and a fountain in the background.

"Well? What do you see, Nan? Do you like it? Is it good? Do you think Mommy will like it? What do you think, Buskers?" Maddy scratches her dog's crooked ear before slowly turning her head toward Nan and eyeing her evenly. "What do *you* think, Nan?"

Nan gazes at her granddaughter. Her raven-black hair frames inquisitive green eyes, and her upturned nose houses a small family of freckles.

"I think you have captured a wonderful image worthy of framing, and your mommy is going to be very, very pleased with her Christmas present this year." Nan hugs Maddy, and they both appraise her work of art.

"It's Buskers, you know—Buskers in the park running near the fountain—and there is a family having a picnic, watching him. Will you help me frame it? Can we go to your gallery and frame it nicely, pleeeaasse?"

Nan winces at the image of the family; the three of them look very much like Maddy, her mom, and her absent father. Nan doesn't harbour any ill will toward her former son-in-law, for she knows relationships are hard work. However, it pains her to see Maddy missing him so. Nan knows that her daughter is also grieving the loss of her marriage, but Cherrie is resilient and her work at the university keeps her focused.

"Of course we'll frame it at the gallery. Think about what colour of matte and frame you'd like to use. We can do it tomorrow morning if you like. Now, what should we have for dinner, Miss Maddy? Crocodile stew or pigeon pie tonight?"

"Oh, Nan," giggles Maddy. "We ate that last night! I think dinosaur fingers and chips, and then later after dinner, can you tell me a story, pleeeaaasssee?"

"Okay, if you insist, Miss Maddy, but only after we tidy up after dinner and take Buskers for a quick walky."

Dozing in his basket, Buskers' tail wags as the words "Buskers" and "walky" echo through his canine brain.

AS NAN and Maddy stroll down Rupert Lane, Buskers sniffs along the trees and hedges. The cedar boughs sway in the mild evening breeze. Nan loves early autumn evenings, when daylight lingers and she can hear families talking as they eat their grilled dinners outside.

"Nan," Maddy says softly, breaking the silence, "I love living here with you and Buskers and Mom. I wanna stay here forever!"

Nan squeezes Maddy's hand and they head farther up the lane.

As they pass Mr. Rupert's house, Nan notices a shadow in the window and gives a hearty wave. The figure jerks slightly, and slowly a hand waves back at them. Nan smiles. Winning over Mr. Rupert is taking longer than anticipated, yet she has time on her side—more than he has on his.

Nan thinks about the first time she set eyes on their home. She clearly remembers following the curving lane to a small crescent with seven uniquely styled homes. They were not luxurious, but they were charming. Each home had its own architectural bent, yet they seemed to share a kinship to each other, like blood relations.

The original builder was frugal, yet his handmade craftsmanship stood the test of time. The long-retired developer of this small enclave still lives in the second-to-last house on the lane. Despite his failing eyesight and hearing and his gnarled, arthritic bones, he keeps a keen watch on *his* neighbourhood. The street even bears his surname—Rupert Lane.

Five years ago, Mr. Rupert watched when the house at 113 Rupert Lane went on the market. Within a few days it sold, and he wondered who his new neighbours would be. It wasn't long before he peered out of his living room window one morning to see a moving van out front. A middle-aged woman appeared with an odd-looking dog at her side. As she directed the movers, Mr. Rupert strained to see her face. "She's not unattractive," he mumbled to himself. "She's not a youngster, but she isn't an oldster like me either." A much younger woman walked up to her with a toddler clinging to her side.

"Hmm..." hummed Mr. Rupert as he noted all three of his new neighbours' raven-coloured hair. "A family of crows has moved in next door." Having Scottish and Métis ancestry, Mr. Rupert had, over time, simply stopped connecting with his Métis heritage. Yet, there he was, wistfully recalling the voice of his cherished grandmother singing to him in Michif—a mixture of French and Cree—when he was a young lad.

Nearing the end of their walk, Nan notices smoke from their neighbour's grill and watches its shadows melting into the cooling evening. She watches Maddy, whose usual happy, open expression is suddenly serious, and it reminds Nan of another young girl, whose sepia-coloured photograph lies buried in a desk drawer. Nan shivers as she ushers Maddy and Buskers indoors.

## CHAPTER TWO

# Two Sisters from Daylu

WITH THE Beatles playing in the background—"Yellow Submarine" is one of Maddy's favourites—Maddy and Nan settle into the cushy loveseat with a bowl of lightly salted popcorn. Despite her daughter's protests, Nan tends to indulge Maddy. It is a grandmother's right to spoil her grandchild, and she sees no harm in it. In fact, she relishes in it.

"Okay, is everyone comfy now? What story would you like to hear this evening?"

Maddy puts her index finger to pursed lips and thinks for a minute. "Nan, can you tell me the story about that old, crinkled photograph with the two little girls?"

During the summer, Maddy discovered the photograph tucked away in Nan's desk. Maddy is curious about the image of two young girls standing close together. The taller girl has her dark hair tied back and is obviously older than the shorter girl with braided hair. They each have a blanket—the older girl carries hers on her arm and the younger one has hers wrapped around her shoulders. Their feet are covered in soft moccasins. Their cheeks are plump. Their eyes glance suspiciously at the camera. Maddy asked her mother about the photograph, and Cherrie told her to ask her grandmother. When she asked Nan, she said she would tell Maddy one day when she had more time. Maddy wonders if Nan has enough time now.

"Did you ever meet the girls in the wrinkly photograph?" inquires Maddy.

Nan musters a smile. "No, my dear, I never met the girls in the photograph, but I do know some things about them."

She squeezes Maddy's hand and closes her eyes briefly. It is important for her granddaughter to know this story, yet she feels uneasy sharing it. Nan takes a deep breath and begins.

"A long, long time ago, there were two little girls who were sisters. The elder sister's name was Mac-kinnay and the younger sister was Beep. They were very close, and Beep looked up to her big sister a lot. Their mother,

Yanima, and their father, Long, named them. They lived far away in the north on the BC-Yukon border. They were Kaska Dena people.

"Now, names are a funny thing and can change throughout one's life. Certain people believe that names should be earned and honoured as one goes through life. So it's possible that Elders might have given Mac-kinnay and Beep different names as they grew up."

"Do you think my name will change one day, Nan?" asks Maddy.

"Well, it may or it may not. It kind of depends on how your life unfolds. I hope not, because I would miss calling you Maddy, my sweet. But today, I bet you could keep your old name with your new name."

"Okay, I'll have to think about that," Maddy says seriously.

"One day, a tall man dressed in a long black robe came into Mac-kinnay and Beep's community, which was called Daylu," Nan tells Maddy, pointing to a map she laid out on her lap. He gathered the community together. 'From this day forward, all community members must be baptized into the Catholic Church and everyone will be given new names,' he announced in broken Kaska."

"Why did they need new names?" asks Maddy. "And what does 'baptized' mean again?"

"Hmmm ... good questions. First of all, I believe the Catholic Church felt they had to convert as many 'Indians'—as they were called then—to the Catholic faith. So, this meant that priests and missionaries were sent to isolated First Nations communities to spread their religious beliefs. I think the Church changed their names for different reasons. One was to cut their connection to their old ways and beliefs and to make them think more like Christians. And baptism is a cleansing ritual to transform you into a Christian."

"What old beliefs?" asks Maddy.

"Well, the Kaska Dena people needed to live in harmony with nature in order to survive. So, I believe they embraced an Indigenous belief system that greatly respected nature and the spirits that provided things they needed—like animals for fur and meat, and forests for homes and tools, and plants for food and medicine."

"Oh, I remember my teacher telling us once that some people give thanks to a tree's spirit when they cut it down. Is that what you mean, Nan?"

"Yes, that's exactly what I mean, Maddy. You're very clever, you know," Nan says, smiling at how quickly

Maddy catches on. "Also, the priests and the nuns didn't want the Kaska Dena people speaking their own language because they didn't understand what they were saying. Of course, it was easier for them to remember and pronounce English names, but just as importantly, I think they wanted them to stop thinking in the old ways. It's hard to explain, but the language people speak tells us something about how they think about the world. Anyway, the priests and nuns thought their beliefs were better and that English was more civilized than Indigenous languages."

"Hmm... I need to think about that too, Nan. I don't know any other language, so I guess I don't know whether English is better."

"That's an interesting way to think about it," Nan replies. "How can any of us know if something is better or worse if we don't really know what it is?

"Before long, Mac-kinnay and Beep's family were baptized together, and their new names were entered into the Holy Family Mission church records. The baptism took place many years ago, on a summer day on August 1, 1925. The black-robed priest changed their names: Mac-kinnay was now called Agnes, and Beep was called Martha. Neither girl liked her new name, so quietly they renamed themselves Aggie and Mudgy."

"Oh, I like the names Aggie and Mudgy," whispers Maddy.

"Me too," says Nan. "A couple of years went by, and Aggie and Mudgy got used to their names, though their parents, Long and Yanima, still called them by their old names when no one else was around.

"Then one day, Long had a bad hunting accident and died. Aggie and Mudgy missed their father terribly. They were learning that life could be very harsh. Of course, they were very sad, but life was especially hard for Yanima, who had to raise the family on her own. Aggie and Mudgy's older brother, Sylvestor, was there to assist his mother, and everyone in the community helped too, but it was still difficult. Yanima was slowly getting used to carrying on without Long when another priest came into the community.

This priest was tall with a narrow build, mousy brown hair, and a pale complexion. There was something harsh and stern about him, and he had an intense look in his eyes. People were afraid of him."

"Why were the people afraid?" asks Maddy.

"Perhaps they sensed the Church was forcing them to change their ways of being, and they didn't know or understand what was happening or why. The people observed that he was powerful and that it was related to him wearing the robes of a Catholic priest."

"It doesn't sound very good that one person could upset a whole community," says Maddy. "What was his name?"

"I totally agree with you about that, my dear. The priest's name was Father Allard."

"Oh, I wonder if he had to change his name too? Maybe Aggie and Mudgy gave him a nickname like White Raven, 'cause he wore black all the time."

"Perhaps they did," muses Nan, smiling to herself.

"Soon after Father Allard's arrival in late spring, he told Yanima that the girls had to go away to school. 'I will take them to their new school, Yanima,' he said. 'They will learn to read and write and to worship our Almighty God.' Yanima just nodded. She was afraid—afraid of Father Allard and also fearful for the future. All of her friends and relatives were afraid of Father Allard too; she just didn't know how to stand up to him. I'm sure she was heartbroken knowing that Aggie and Mudgy would soon be taken from her. She loved them very much, and with Long gone, they were more important to her than ever."

"I wonder what Aggie and Mudgy thought about all of this. And why couldn't they go to school near their home?" asks Maddy.

"In those days, there wasn't a school in their community, but there was a school in Whitehorse. It was much closer than the school that the priest took them to, so I really don't know why they had to go so very far away from home. There are a lot of mysteries about how and why things happened the way they did."

"That's for sure," Maddy cries, crossing her arms indignantly. "If someone came to take me away to school, I'd run and hide where no one could find me!"

"And I would make sure they didn't find you too," Nan says while giving Maddy a warm hug.

"Finally, the day came in July when the priest took Aggie and Mudgy away. Yanima could not bear to see the girls depart, so their brother Sylvestor, along with their grandmother Gyuss and other women from the community, saw them off at the edge of the river.

"'Aggie, take care of Mudgy on your journey,' Gyuss whispered in Kaska to her oldest granddaughter as they waited for the boat to pick them up on the riverbank. 'Use your wits and do your best to keep her—and yourself—safe.'"

Nan sighs.

"Try and imagine what it would be like, Maddy, watching the girls get into the riverboat, with Father

Allard barking at them to sit still so he could get in without tripping on his long black robe."

"It would have been funny if he fell into the river, wouldn't it, Nan?"

"Yes, that would have been funny, though not very nice, Maddy," Nan says, chuckling. "I don't believe anyone on that riverbank was smiling much that day. Remember that Aggie was the same age as you are now, and she was responsible for her younger sister too."

Maddy puts her fingers to her Nan's lips, her eyes wide. "I would be very, very afraid, Nan."

"Yes, I'm sure both girls were scared, but at least they had each other," Nan says. "I think Mudgy held on to Aggie as tight as she could while their grandmother and brother watched the boat slice along the riverbank, the outboard noisily disturbing the peace of the water. As the boat reached the confluence of the Laird and Dease Rivers, the passengers were just tiny specks in the distance. That was where they lost sight of them. The heartbroken little group on the shore trudged back to their homes. No one knew if they would ever see the girls again."

Maddy frowns and looks up at her grandmother. "And what about Aggie and Mudgy? Do you think they were crying, Nan? I think I would be crying. You and Mommy won't ever send me far away to school, will you?"

"No, my love, never," Nan reassures her. "But one day you may leave us to go to a university in another city."

"I don't think Buskers would like it if I left him to go far away to university, but maybe he could come and visit me. Just imagine, Buskers in university," giggles Maddy.

Buskers' eyelids flicker open at the sound of his name, but he quickly goes back to sleep in his basket. Nan and Maddy giggle when they notice his back legs twitching furiously.

"Maybe he's dreaming that he's running to rescue Aggie and Mudgy from Father Allard," Maddy says. "Go, Buskers, go!"

## CHAPTER THREE

# The River Journey Begins

FOLLOWING A brief break, Nan and Maddy reposition themselves on the plush loveseat. Nan carefully places her cup of peppermint tea on a coaster next to Maddy's apple juice on the side table.

"Now, where was I? Oh, yes, the river journey. Aggie and Mudgy grew up on the Liard River and had great respect for it, as all Kaska Dena people understood the importance of the river from a very early age. It provided sustenance for the Kaska Dena: water, food, and transportation. However, like all mighty rivers, it was also dangerous.

"The Liard River is temperamental. Depending upon the season, it can be a frozen ice surface or a frothing, flood-prone force. The Liard can be quietly deceptive, for it has strong undercurrents. If man or beast falls in, in certain areas, they will probably drown. You have to pay attention at all times and be on the lookout for all sorts of hazards, like low-hanging branches and snags—logs caught in the river.

"The priest didn't know anything about navigating rivers, let alone the Liard River, so he hired two Indigenous brothers to transport them to the far side of Dease Lake. The guides came from Dease Lake and were known as the Dick brothers. Their flat-bottomed vessel was ideal for transporting freight and people between northern communities. Despite being in their early twenties, they were highly experienced in navigating rivers and setting up camps. More importantly, the brothers were friendly, loved to joke, and were happiest while out on the river."

"Why didn't they just drive to their school? How come they had to go by riverboat?"

"In those days, there wasn't a road. The local people travelled via river routes or by foot along established trails, as they had done for generations. Occasionally, bush planes flew in the northern regions, but they weren't easily accessible to the locals. In fact, it wasn't until the 1940s, during the Second World War, that a highway was built that crossed through the small community of Watson Lake, in the Yukon. It was very close to Daylu, which is also known as Lower Post, in BC. "That reminds me. It wasn't just people's names that were changed in those days. They changed the names of communities and mountains and rivers too. The Kaska Dena always knew Daylu as a gathering place where Aggie and Mudgys' ancestors and family lived. It only became known as Lower Post in the late 1800s, after Europeans established a trading post there."

"Do you think Aggie and Mudgy were upset, Nan? Do you think they asked the priest to take them back?"

"I think the girls were quite sad to leave their family and the only home they had known. But at least they had each other, and maybe they thought it would be an adventure. Besides, they were most likely too shy and overwhelmed with their journey, so I suspect they wouldn't have dared say anything to the priest. They were familiar with the environment and knew their guides. It was still their territory, so the landscape and the Dick brothers may have helped put them at ease.

"I like to think that they passed the time on the river by noticing the scenery, watching for rapids, and maybe playing games as to what they could see on shore. Purple patches of slender fireweed line the riverbanks with vibrant splashes of colour in the summer months.

I imagine that rounding a bend in the river, Aggie and Mudgy would guess what they might see: maybe some more wildflowers and wild berries, or perhaps a mama bear and her cubs, a moose and her calf, or even a fox drinking at the river's edge."

"That sounds magical, Nan. How long were they on the riverboat?"

"It took six full days, travelling by day and camping at night. Just imagine how bright the stars in the sky would appear to Aggie and Mudgy, for there were no bright city lights to interfere with the nightly constellations. The stars helped Aggie and Mudgy's ancestors by guiding them home when they were lost. The Kaska Dena saw elements of their origins in the nightly skies. Yanima and Long used to point to the sky and show the girls where to search for bear, moose, wolf trails, and thunderbirds. They especially loved showing their children the aurora borealis, or northern lights, in the winter. The winter night sky lit up in electric colours as their Elders spoke of spirit guides dancing toward the next world."

"Oh, I wish we could see the night sky light up with colours," says Maddy wistfully.

"I'm sure one day you will, sweetie."

"When they came ashore, the Dick brothers quickly set up camp. They let the girls explore while keeping a discrete eye out for them. The girls explored nearby and looked for smooth river stones. The flies and mosquitos didn't seem to bother the girls or their guides. However, flies as thick and black as the priest's robe hovered continually around his face as he swatted at them in vain. The guides roasted fish for the travellers. They ate Dolly Varden, which is like trout—which you like."

"Dolly Varden . . . sounds like the name of a doll! Two names for a fish. That's funny, Nan!"

"Yes, it is unusual for a fish to have a first and last name, but there you are again with the name thing. I don't think Aggie and Mudgy's family members called this fish Dolly Varden. They called it by another name, a Kaska Dena name.

"Anyhow, I'm sure the girls enjoyed the roasted fish. It was so fresh and must have been delicious cooked over an open fire. They were used to a diet of fish, as well as moose, caribou, and mountain sheep. Gathering seasonal bounty such as plants, roots, and wild berries was a nutritional and tasty addition to their diet.

"One day on their journey, they noticed a huge patch of red on shore and realized it was a gigantic patch of wild raspberries. Their guides pulled ashore, and they had a sweet time gorging on raspberries. Aggie and Mudgy lamented the fact that they did not have their birch-bark baskets with them to fill with berries for the journey. What a waste leaving all those berries behind!"

"What does lamented mean again, Nan?"

"It means they were very sorry. Their birch-bark baskets would have been useful for carrying berries with them on their journey."

"Aggie and Mudgy must have had fun eating all those berries. Do wild raspberries taste like our raspberries?" Maddy asks.

"They are a little bit sweeter but smaller and ever so yummy. Hmmm ... I wonder if we have any raspberry ice cream left?"

"Let's check," grins Maddy.

As Nan fills two bowls with raspberry ice cream, the front door opens and closes. A woman in her early thirties walks in with a leather briefcase and one bag of groceries. Cherrie is home.

Maddy rushes to give her mom a huge hug.

"How was school today?" Nan asks her daughter. "Did you manage to keep your students at bay?"

"Oh, the usual suspects kept me late, but nothing too draining—though it is good to be home. Oooh ... any of that ice cream left?" she asks.

Maddy tugs at her mother's sleeve. "Mommy, Nan's telling me the story about the old photograph with the two girls—Aggie and Mudgy. We were just where the girls are on the riverboat and are going to eat wild raspberries beside the river."

Cherrie gives her mom a level glance. "Oh, that's a good story, but a long one. Maybe you should continue it tomorrow, kiddo."

"Oh, Mom . . . Can't I hear it all tonight? Pleeeaasse."

"Madeleine. Tomorrow is another day with time for more storytelling," Cherrie replies. "It is late, so now it's time for bath and bed!"

"All right, just as soon as I finish my ice cream."

Nan hands Cherrie her own bowl of ice cream and re-heats the kettle for tea. Maddy clinks her spoon on her empty bowl and dramatically shuffles down the hall to get ready for bath and bed. Buskers' nails go *click, click, click* after her.

NAN PLACES the peppermint tea near the teapot and waits for her daughter to begin the conversation.

"Oh, I can't wait for reading break," Cherrie sighs. "I need some time away from work. I want to spend time with Maddy, without constantly rushing about."

"Cherrie, I am so proud of you. Just think, you are on the road to a tenure track position at one of the best universities on the west coast. You should be very proud of yourself."

"Thanks, Mom. You remember I have a conference tomorrow. Is it all right if Maddy hangs out with you, or should I book her into the community rec centre for half the day?"

"Oh, no problem. We have a project at the gallery to attend to, and then I suspect Saturday lunch at Nita's may be on the agenda. At some point, I'm sure Maddy will ask me to continue the tale of Aggie and Mudgy."

"Right," says Cherrie. "So, how is the story going? How deeply are you presenting things to Maddy?"

Nan observes dark shadows under her daughter's eyes. It must be the pressure of work and the strain of her separation from Maddy's father. Yet, Cherrie has charisma and carries herself with assurance. Nan knows she's biased, but there's a certain mystique about her daughter that is very attractive.

"Maddy needs to hear the truth. Children are very intuitive, and Maddy is especially so. Look at you. I couldn't get away with shabby story lines when you were a youngster."

Cherrie laughs. "Yeah, I know, but don't you think I grew up with thicker skin? Maddy is bright, but not nearly as tough as me."

Nan pauses and looks Cherrie in the eye. "Maddy is sensitive, yes. But she's stronger than you give her credit for."

"You think so? Well, that's good. Goodness knows, girls need to be tough today."

Nan nods in agreement.

"Oh, by the way," Cherrie says. "I think it's time for another pie for Mr. Rupert. He actually *waved* to me in the driveway this evening."

"Yes, he is thawing, albeit at a glacial pace," chuckles Nan.

"He seems less suspicious of us now, though I can't shake the sense he harbours strange ideas about us, as if we're a coven of witches."

Mother and daughter giggle at the notion of themselves as witches. Out of the blue, Cherrie pushes herself away from the table, grabs a broom and starts riding it around the kitchen, one hand held high, as if she's balancing a pie. Nan laughs and laughs.

They both know that Mr. Rupert was surprised and delighted when they sent him a blueberry pie the other week, but they didn't expect the note he left with the clean pie plate on their front porch the following day. It read: "Thank you kindly for the pie. If in the future you see the need to repeat this offering, please note that blueberry stains my dentures, but apple doesn't. Regards, L. Rupert."

"My, it's good to laugh," says Nan, pouring her daughter some tea, "but I think Mr. Rupert is lonely. Maybe his loneliness reinforces misleading ideas about other people. But yes, you're right. We'll pick up some Spartans tomorrow and get it right this time."

Cherrie cradles the mug with her long, elegant fingers and appraises her mother. Grey is beginning to dominate her thick head of hair, but she's still got oodles of energy and enthusiasm. Cherrie was afraid that Nan would lose her joyfulness when her husband died over a decade ago, but she needn't have worried. Nan is living life to its fullest, and having Maddy around helps to keep them both young at heart.

Cherrie sips her tea quietly. *I don't know what I'd do without her, especially with the separation,* she thinks. Giving a thumbs up, Cherrie flashes her mother a big grin. "Mmmm ... awesome cup of tea, Mom."

## CHAPTER FOUR

# The Journey Overland, Dease Lake to Telegraph Creek

NAN, MADDY, and Buskers pile out of the four-door sedan and enter through the back door into Aksak Gallery, a small but vibrant art gallery located near Granville Island. It's a busy part of Vancouver, and Maddy loves all the hustle and bustle of the area. The gallery is a godsend to Nan, and despite the challenges of running a small business, she loves the people and art associated with it. So does Maddy. She wanders around to look at the art on the walls, often asking questions about the artists. And of course, the staff fuss over Maddy and her artwork.

Nan and Maddy go to the back room of the gallery, where a selection of finished frames and mattes in various sizes and colours are stored. Maddy knows to look for colours that match or complement the colours in her painting, and she quickly finds a brightly painted frame the exact right shade of yellow. It's a bit big, but Nan finds a pale purple matte to go around the painting and cuts it down to fit the frame perfectly.

"What do you think, my dear?" inquires Nan, holding the painting with the matte and frame up to the light, making sure there are no fingerprints or dust on the glass before she secures the backing.

"I love it, Nan," Maddy beams. "Do you think Mommy will like it? I love the purple matting and the yellow frame. We made good choices, didn't we, Nan? I bet Mommy is gonna be surprised with this under our Christmas tree!"

"She will love it. I'm sure of it. How about we stop by Nita's Restaurant on the way home for lunch? Buskers can snooze in the car, and maybe he'll get a little something from Nita's as a treat if he behaves."

"Oh, Nan. Buskers always behaves. He's a gentlemanly dog," laughs Maddy.

Nan and Maddy are regulars at Nita's. Nan has fond memories of dining there when Cherrie was a young girl and wants to carry on this tradition with her granddaughter. The original owner—Nita—is a good-natured woman who always welcomed Nan warmly; Nita is now retired but occasionally comes into the restaurant to greet her customers. The server hands them two sets of crayons and paper placemats to doodle on while waiting for their food.

One of Maddy's works hangs on the restaurant wall that is reserved for their clients' masterpieces. It's another brightly coloured picture of Maddy and Nan walking Buskers along Rupert Lane. After ordering their lunch, with an extra burger—no bun—for Buskers, the pair settles in with their crayons.

While carefully drawing with a teal crayon, Maddy asks: "Nan, do you think Aggie and Mudgy ever went out for lunch with their granny?"

"Well, I suppose it depends on what you mean by going 'out' for lunch. Remember, they lived in an isolated northern community, so their meals came from the river and the land. Restaurants didn't exist, but they may have hiked to places to gather food and taken meals along with them."

"Hmmm ... I see. When we left the story, the girls were eating berries and wishing they had their birchbark baskets to carry along. I guess that's kind of like going out for a treat, isn't it?"

Nan smiles and nods softly.

"I wonder if they thought about what Yanima would have made if they'd been able to bring those berries home. They wouldn't want to waste them, would they?"

"No, they wouldn't. Good thinking, Maddy," Nan says. "Yanima might have dried the berries so they could be added to meat and fat to become pemmican, which lasts a long time and is a good source of energy. Blueberries were also a favourite. Abundant blueberry patches were coveted by all the families—including the bear families!"

"PEMM-I-CAN! I like that word. I wonder if I would like how it tastes?" muses Maddy.

Nan studies the little dark head sitting across from her. "We can pick up the story while we're waiting for lunch if you like."

"Yes, please!"

"Okay, let's do that. Several days after the raspberry feast, the riverboat left the Dease River and entered a long body of water called Dease Lake. The travellers camped here overnight. The next day they travelled fifty kilometres along the lake to a tiny community called— can you guess its name?—Dease Lake!"

"Do you think they liked Dease Lake, Nan?"

"Perhaps, but they weren't there very long. It was here they had to say goodbye to their guides. The Dick brothers had been Aggie and Mudgy's source of comfort and security along the river journey. The brothers each gave Aggie and Mudgy a small bird that they had been carving on the trip. As they watched the brothers return to their riverboat, Aggie and Mudgy clutched their little wooden birds tightly; they already missed the brothers' familiar faces, their easy laughter, and caring manner."

"With the riverboat journey over, the girls had travelled just over three hundred kilometres from their homeland. The next stage of their journey would be overland. The closest community to Dease Lake is eighty kilometres away and is called Telegraph Creek. Back then there wasn't a local bus or train running between the communities, so Aggie and Mudgy and the priest caught a ride in a mail truck, which delivered mail between Dease Lake and Telegraph Creek."

"Why was it called Telegraph Creek, Nan?"

"Before telephones, something called a telegram was a form of communication that could travel quickly between places. A very long time ago—during the 1860s—this little community was important as a staging point for two overland telegraph lines. The region was opening up to resource development like mining and forestry, so people needed a way to communicate that was faster than the mail truck. It seemed like almost overnight the area was busy with surveyors and construction workers, who needed supplies. It all contributed to the creation of Telegraph Creek. Anyway, guess how long it took Aggie and Mudgy to travel the eighty kilometres from Dease Lake to Telegraph Creek?"

"I don't know. Two hours?"

"Nope, it took all day to drive along a winding, narrow, and bumpy dirt road. It wouldn't surprise me if the roads made the girls feel queasy, but I bet they couldn't help but notice the striking vistas of mountains, forests, and river valleys along the way. At a high section on the road, the truck driver stopped and let all the passengers out. He pointed to a section of rock caves across the river valley that was home to wild mountain goats. Aggie and Mudgy could see white shapes hopping from one big rock to the next on the steep cliffs."

"I imagine their small faces perked up once they started down a steep incline and saw a modest town built along another river—the massive Stikine River. And unbeknownst to them, they were to remain in Telegraph Creek for three weeks!"

"Three whole weeks! How come?"

"At the time, the town was building a Catholic church in Telegraph Creek, and the priest came to help. Now

Aggie and Mudgy didn't know anything about building churches, so happily for them, they were allowed to go off on their own. As long as they returned at dinnertime, they were safe from trouble."

"One day, the girls scrambled up a nearby hill and found a big patch of Saskatoon berries. They loved Saskatoon berries! They played a game where they were going to surprise their family with a feast of berries, and picked and ate until they were covered in the purple-blue berry juice. It was so much fun and reminded them of being back in Daylu, where they often went berry picking with their mother. Of course, they lost track of time.

"Suddenly, Aggie looked up and noticed that the sun was getting lower in the sky. With a start, she realized they were late for the dinner hour. They scurried back down the hill and ran as fast as they could to their lodgings. Father Allard was waiting for them when they got to the door. They could tell that he was very angry by the look in his eyes, his clenched mouth, and his tightly wound fists."

Nan pauses to sip her tea and looks across at Maddy. Her small hand remains intently coiled around a crimson crayon. "My God," Nan whispers to herself. "I'm choking on my words."

In a low voice, Nan says, "Maddy, Father Allard treated Aggie and Mudgy very badly. In his fury, he grabbed them by the hair and threw them to the floor. He kicked them over and over again. Then he pulled off the girls' berry-stained clothes and tossed their small bodies into a tub of water. The girls must have been in shock as they washed themselves in a daze. The priest stared from a distance, adding to the sisters' distress. Deep feelings of shame overcame them."

"Why was he so mean to them?" Maddy quietly asks, looking up from her doodling.

"I guess because they didn't do as they were told," Nan says.

"But that's not fair. They didn't do it on purpose, and they weren't really being bad, just forgetful."

"I know, Maddy. It seems incredible that a grown man, let alone a priest, could act so violently toward children."

Maddy drops her crayon and looks straight at her Nan. "Didn't Aggie or Mudgy yell or scream for help?"

"No, they were all alone with him, in a tiny, isolated community, far from home. If anyone overheard the commotion, they probably wouldn't have dared stand up to Father Allard. Remember, he had an unkind heart and could be mean-spirited to everyone. That's the way it was: he just didn't have a good heart inside of him, and Aggie and Mudgy suffered because of this."

"He shouldn't have been a priest, should he, Nan?"

"No, he shouldn't have, Maddy. Unfortunately, there were other priests just like him during that time. They couldn't respect different people and cultures, and if the children didn't obey, some priests and nuns could be very cruel."

"I think I would run away," Maddy says, pumping her small fist on the table.

"As a matter of fact, that's exactly what Aggie thought they should do. She felt terrible that she hadn't been able to protect her little sister from the beating, so the next morning she told Mudgy her plan. They were going to run away from that priest and go back home where they would be safe. The day before, Aggie had noticed a shortcut out of town, so they quietly slipped outside without anyone noticing.

"Aggie led Mudgy by the hand toward the main road back to Dease Lake. The girls walked a fair distance on the dirt road when they came across a Tahltan family heading toward Telegraph Creek. The Kaska and Tahltan languages originate from a single Dené language family, so even though their dialects were different, they could understand each other.

"'Where are you heading, little ones?' asked the concerned father.

"'The priest is taking us too far away to school, and we can't see our family. We need to get back to Daylu right away!' said a determined Aggie.

"'Aaach, they have no right, no right,' cursed the woman as she spat a dark wad of tobacco on the ground. Her young child shyly looked at Aggie and Mudgy with huge brown eyes.

"Hoping they could help, Mudgy bravely spoke. 'We have to go back to Yanima. She wants us home!'

"'Hmmmm...' muttered the father. He looked far past the girls into the wilderness. 'Daylu is a very long way from here.' Slowly, he crouched low to the dirt road, and using his fingers he drew a picture of a grizzly bear and its tracks on the ground.

"'Many big grizzly bears that way,' he said solemnly as he pointed in the direction the girls were heading. The woman nodded her head in agreement.

"'Maybe you should come back to town with us,' smiled the father, extending his hands to each of the girls.

"Aggie and Mudgy stood still in the middle of the road and thought for a long moment. The girls knew that grizzly bears were part of their environment and had to be respected—and avoided. Weighing the pros and cons of continuing on alone, Aggie reluctantly said, 'Okay, we'll go back with you.'"

"Was the priest angry again?" Maddy asks, her dark eyes wide with fear.

"Yes, he was angry again. He threw the girls into bed without dinner, but at least he didn't beat them that day. At the time, it seemed better than confronting grizzly bears. Aggie and Mudgy sat on the edge of the bed and looked out a small window to the streets of the town. Aggie put her arm around Mudgy and whispered, 'We'll find a way back home someday.'"

Just then, a server appears at the table and deftly lays two plates down. With a wink at Maddy, she slides a doggy bag to the side with Buskers' burger treat. Nan agrees to continue the story later at home, and they hungrily tuck into their lunch.

## CHAPTER FIVE

# Telegraph Creek to the Pacific Ocean

NAN PEELS apples while glancing out her kitchen window as Maddy and her buddy Lucas play in the backyard. Lucas is the same age as Maddy, but he's a few inches shorter and has ginger-tinged hair. On weekends, he frequently shows up at Nan's backdoor, looking for Maddy and Buskers. Lucas lives two doors down with his dad and stepmom and envies Maddy because she has a dog.

Nan is grateful for Lucas, as he entices Maddy outdoors to dig for worms and to hunt for banana slugs. Maddy enjoys their adventures and often creates little works of art depicting their days. One such painting highlights a family of banana slugs. The lady slugs are holding pastel parasols, whereas the gentlemen slugs wear red and blue berets. Maddy gave that painting to Lucas, and it hangs on his bedroom wall.

"Hmmm . . . I think some mini-apple pies are in order," Nan says to herself. "Lucas can take one home, and Mr. Rupert will be pleasantly surprised as well."

Later on, Maddy, Lucas, and Buskers bounce into the kitchen. "Ooooh . . . yum! I smell something good," shouts Lucas.

"That's Nan's apple pie. Isn't it a great smell? I wish I could paint that smell . . . hmmm . . . what an idea . . . golden yellow and cinnamon on canvas!" Maddy says dreamily.

"I wish my stepmom could bake. She buys stuff from the grocery store, but it never smells like this," says Lucas.

"Well, Lucas, there is a mini-apple pie with your name on it in the oven. It will be out soon," says Nan.

"THANK YOU, Nan!" beams Lucas.

"While you're waiting, I'll make some cocoa for us," says Nan.

"With marshmallows, please," Maddy says with a grin.

"Would I ever forget marshmallows?" Nan asks, her hands on her hips as she leans toward Maddy.

Maddy catches the twinkle in her Nan's eyes and puts her arms around her grandmother's waist. "I love you, Nan. You always think of everything!"

"Hey, I've got an idea while we're waiting, Nan. Can you continue the story, please?"

"I'm not sure Lucas would be interested," Nan says, looking at the tousled top of his ginger hair.

"Sure I would," exclaims Lucas. "Maddy's told me all about Aggie and Mudgy."

"Has she? And what do you think of the story, Lucas?"

"It's kinda exciting, Nan. It's kinda sad in parts too, but I think it's so cool that they're on an adventure," Lucas replies. "I'd love to be on an adventure in the wilderness, just not with that mean priest!"

Nan chuckles and addresses her small audience: "Okay then. Since everyone is up to speed, let's carry on.

"The girls woke up with long faces the morning after their attempt to escape from Telegraph Creek. Downhearted but resigned to remain, they went down the stairs for breakfast, vowing to stay out of the priest's way. Aggie and Mudgy nibbled quietly on their dry, cold toast and gooey porridge. The meagre breakfast was bland, but they were hungry."

"A thin woman came into the room and barked at them to hurry up and finish their breakfast. She was the churchwarden in Telegraph Creek, a stern French-Canadian woman named Odèle who did as the priest commanded her. The girls soon found out that it was her job to prepare them for 'civilized' society prior to leaving on the next stage of their journey. In a mix of English and broken Kaska, she ordered them to move their chairs away from the table as she approached with long, black-handled scissors. Mudgy started to cry.

"Aggie stood up and faced Odèle. 'What are you doing with those?!' she asked, pointing at the scissors.

"'I'm going to cut your disgusting hair,' Odèle snarled.

"'Our hair is not disgusting,' Aggie yelled, as Odèle shoved her back into her chair.

"'It won't be when I'm done with it,' she said, with a hard hand on the girl's shoulder to keep her still.

"'Fine,' Aggie said. 'I don't care if you cut it all off. It will grow back.' She stiffened her spine and closed her eyes, listening to Mudgy whimpering beside her, determined not to let her feelings show.

"'You're next,' Odèle said, turning to Mudgy as piles of thick black hair fell to the floor in great blobs.

"When she was done, Odèle stood back to appraise her work. Aggie stared at her with cold eyes and turned to Mudgy. Her hair no longer fell over her sister's small shoulders down to her waist. They both had short bobs with bangs cut hard and straight, high up on their foreheads."

"That must have been awful," sighs Maddy. "I wouldn't want my hair cut so short, especially by someone so mean."

Lucas slowly nods his head in agreement.

"Then Odèle told them to get undressed so she could take their old clothes away," Nan says. "Their tenderly mended cotton dresses were supported by buckskin straps that belted around their small waists. A small patch of beaded floral designs was stitched at each end of their belts. Aggie and Mudgy had done the beading on their belts themselves. It was good practice taught by Gyuss. Their grandmother beaded many items. She used seed beads that are made of very small pieces of European-made glass. Her patterns were cut from birch bark and often incorporated floral designs. Her moccasins, gloves, and pouches were well made, and when she could, she traded these items at the Hudson's Bay Company trading store. Gyuss was just beginning to teach Aggie the more difficult moccasin designs when the priest took the girls away.

"Naturally, the girls hated the idea of being naked in front of this woman, but they knew she would have her way, so they slowly undressed and handed her their clothes. It was hard to let go of the comforting smells of wood smoke that lingered in the fabric from the camp-fires the guides had built during the river journey.

"Odèle stuffed the dresses into a bag and threw them into a corner of the room. Then she handed each of them a school uniform, a grey jumper over top a stiff white blouse, along with a drab sweater. She also issued them knee-high stockings and a pair of brown Oxford shoes. Imagine, they had never worn shoes, let alone ones that were so clunky and tight and ugly. Their feet got hot and they hurt. Oh, how they missed the soft moccasins that their granny Gyuss had made for them. Mudgy especially hated shoes for a long time afterward.

"One morning, a few days after their haircuts, Odèle came to their room and coldly stated: "You must keep your new clothes spotless or you will get in trouble. No berry stains! Father Allard will be coming to get you soon, and you'll be on your way from Telegraph Creek."

"What if Aggie and Mudgy had been boys?" asks Lucas.

"Boys would also have been issued uniforms—a pair of long pants, a long-sleeved shirt, Oxford shoes, and a jacket. Their hair would be almost shaven and allowed to grow out in a short style," replies Nan.

"That sounds awful," Lucas says. "I hate wearing a shirt and jacket. It's hard to climb trees in clothes like that!"

"I know," Maddy says. "I don't think they wanted kids to have any fun at all."

"Hang on, your cocoa is ready," Nan interrupts. "Let it cool a bit before you gulp it down. The next stage of their journey involved river travel again. Can you guess which river?"

"Well, it couldn't be the Dease River or the Liard River 'cause that would take them back home, so it must be another river. Which one, Nan?" asks Maddy.

"Remember I mentioned that Telegraph Creek is located on a riverbank? Just a second," says Nan, as she reaches for her leather-bound atlas on the bookshelf. "Yes, here it is. See how the Stikine River flows through northwestern BC and ends up emptying into the sea near the town of Wrangell, Alaska? It's a very long distance, and because it travels across the Canada–US border, it's an international river. Aggie and Mudgy travelled on it all the way from Telegraph Creek to Wrangell."

"Wow, that's a long river. Did they go by sailboat or in a speed boat?" asks Lucas.

"Neither," says Nan.

"Did they travel by canoe or a riverboat like the one they had travelled on before?" asks Maddy.

"Nope."

"Ferry boat?" says Lucas.

"No, they travelled by paddlewheeler boat," says Nan. "Paddlewheelers operated up and down the Stikine River, moving passengers and freight. Just think of Huck Finn and you'll get an idea of what one looks like. Hey, we even have a paddlewheeler here in the city. Remember, Maddy? We saw one sailing by Granville Island. I think it had lots of tourists on board."

"That's right!" says Maddy. "It had a ginormous wheel at the back going around and around in the water. I wonder what Aggie and Mudgy thought of that?"

"They had never seen a paddlewheeler and naturally must have been curious," says Nan. "I imagine they cautiously explored the long vessel. They were used to travel on rivers, but not in a vessel with several decks that carried people and freight. These vessels weren't huge like the BC ferries that travel between Vancouver and Vancouver Island nowadays. They were smaller, with a shallow keel, but could still handle freight and passengers on the river. When the paddlewheeler began to pull away from the dock, Mudgy grabbed Aggie's arm while the vessel shook with vibrations. They covered their ears as the shrill whistle blew and smoke bellowed out of the tall smokestack."

"Oooh... that would be scary if you'd never been on a boat like that before," Maddy says.

"Yeah, but exciting too, don't you think?" asks Lucas.

"How long did the trip take?"

"Hmmm... good question, Lucas. I'm not exactly sure, but I believe the distance by river from Telegraph Creek to Wrangell is about 240 kilometres. That's about as far as a trip from Vancouver to Hope and back.

"And yes, I imagine that Aggie and Mudgy did find the boat rather exciting. They probably watched different-looking people stroll along the decks as they admired the scenery. Everything was new and unfamiliar as the paddlewheeler churned its way through the middle of the great river.

"Farther along the Stikine, Aggie and Mudgy would see huge mountains covered with snow on their peaks. Though they didn't know what they were seeing at the time, the girls saw big and small glaciers tucked in between the mountains. The lower Stikine River flows by the Stikine Icecap, where they likely saw the Great Glacier. This huge glacier reached the Stikine riverbank a decade before Aggie and Mudgy's journey. Sadly, over the years, the Great Glacier has been receding faster than we'd like because of global warming."

"Cool, I'd love to see a glacier!" exclaims Lucas.

"Me too!" says Maddy. "Especially before they shrink too much."

"They are spectacular to see and very loud when calving," adds Nan.

"What's calving, Nan?" asks Maddy.

"That's when a large chunk of ice breaks off of a glacier and falls into a lake or ocean. It's quite dramatic to witness," replies Nan.

"Approaching the mouth of the Stikine River, the vessel had to cross the ocean channel, approximately twelve kilometres, to reach Wrangell, Alaska. As they came into Wrangell Harbor, they would have seen men of all shapes and sizes working on the docks, hauling materials, hollering to each other as they laboured. A long time ago, in the late 1890s, Wrangell was a very busy port of call. The reason for this was because of gold. Gold fever gripped North America as gold was discovered in the Yukon. Due to gold fever, Wrangell thrived as thousands of men travelled up to the Yukon, seeking their fortune.

"When Aggie and Mudgy arrived in Wrangell, the port was busy but nothing like in the gold rush era. Sailing in, the girls would have been among many different watercrafts—canoes, fishing boats, paddlewheelers, and steamships. And everywhere they looked, there were fish canneries."

"It must have been thrilling," Maddy says, thinking also of the time when her teacher took her class down to the docks at Vancouver's port.

"Do you think they were allowed to look around the harbour?" asks Lucas.

"They had a short stay in Wrangell before the next leg of their journey. The day they arrived, it was a bit dreary. A misty rain was falling. The girls most likely wondered why the air smelled differently, for it was the first time they had seen the ocean. Imagine that. One thing they would have noticed were some very tall totem poles in Wrangell. Wrangell is in the traditional territory of the Tlingit People, who are well known for their totem carving.

"As Aggie and Mudgy walked down the dock near the main street in Wrangell—Front Street—they stopped at the base of two very tall totem monuments.

"'Aggie, look way up—sooo tall! So many creatures!' said Mudgy in awe.

"Circling the base of the totems, Aggie stretched her neck backwards and said, 'Uncle has talked of these totems. He worked in a cannery one summer and told us stories about creatures carved one on top of another in the pole. Look, I think I see a beaver's teeth, and an eagle's claws and beak at the top of this one. Maybe that is a raven's beak and a man with a tall ringed hat on top of this other one. We will have to ask Uncle when we get home.'

"As soon as the words were out of her mouth, Aggie realized that she didn't know when she would see Uncle or any of her relatives again. I imagine her spirits fell a little at the thought.

"After a brief walkabout, Father Allard ordered the girls to stay close as they needed to clear customs. Needless to say, Aggie and Mudgy probably wanted to keep looking for more totems. I've seen them, and they are quite spectacular," says Nan.

"Didn't they have totems in Daylu, Nan?" asks Maddy.

"No, they didn't. Giant cedar trees don't grow in Kaska Dena territory, so they couldn't carve totem poles like the Tlinglit. That part of the country near the ocean is called a rainforest—just like in Vancouver, except that there are only a few forests left in the city now. Kaska Dena territory is inland, where birch and spruce trees grow, which the people used in other ways, such as making houses, toboggans, snowshoes, drums, and smaller carvings," replies Nan.

"Maddy, remember when we visited the Museum of Anthropology at the university where your mother works? We saw lots of birch-bark baskets, old carving tools such as adzes, and beautiful beadwork on animal hides. These are items that many Indigenous Peoples made and used for generations in the territory that Aggie and Mudgy came from. Many birch-bark baskets had geometric shapes etched on them. Clothing made from hides had colourful beadwork stitched on, just like the beading that Gyuss sewed onto Aggie and Mudgy's moccasins. The tiny colourful beads came from trade with Europeans, but the Kaska Dena also traded with other nations for things like seashells and blue glass beads from Russia."

"Yeah, I also remember some really cool carved horns that came from sheep, right, Nan? They shone so prettily in the light. And I'll never forget all those moccasins and mitts and stuff, decorated with teeny-weeny shiny beads. It must've taken, like, forever to do!"

"So, where did they go next? Did they get back on the paddlewheeler?" asks Lucas.

"No, they didn't get back on the paddlewheeler. As I mentioned, Wrangell is in Alaska, so they had to clear American customs. The customs officer studied them briefly, asked Father Allard a quick question or two, and waved them through. I suspect he didn't want to question the priest's authority."

Before Nan could continue her narrative, the telephone rings. It's Lucas's stepmom asking him to come home for dinner. Nan wraps his warm little apple pie and tells him to walk carefully home with it. Maddy promises to keep Lucas updated on the Aggie and Mudgy saga.

"Well, Miss Maddy, I think we need to attend to some of our own dinner fixings. While I start some prep work for dinner, will you kindly take two of these small pies over to Mr. Rupert?" asks Nan with a direct look at her granddaughter.

"Oh, Nan, do I have to right now?" moans Maddy. She finds Mr. Rupert somewhat crusty and would rather avoid him. Yet in her eight-year-old wisdom, she also knows that Mr. Rupert is a lonely old soul, and somehow he needs apple pies more than she does.

"Hop to it, chick," responds Nan in her no-nonsense voice. "Right now, please and thank you."

"Okaaayyy, I'll go now," says Maddy as she carefully holds up the apple pies.

Nan watches Maddy meander over to Mr. Rupert's house. Buskers sniffs along behind her. The telephone rings again. This time it's Cherrie. Her conference has wrapped up, and she's invited for dinner with some of the delegates. Nan assures her that all is well, and quietly gives thanks for all that she has.

## CHAPTER SIX

# Wrangell to Prince Rupert

NAN FEELS a cold nose on her lower leg and realizes that Buskers is telling her something. It's five o'clock, and being a creature of habit, Buskers never forgets to remind Nan when it's dinnertime. "Okay, my old friend, doggy dinner du jour coming up," coos Nan as she strokes Buskers' head.

As Buskers noisily crunches his chow, Maddy runs into the kitchen holding a bright, multi-coloured scarf. "What do you have there, Missy?" inquires Nan.

"Mr. Rupert gave it to me!" says Maddy with an impish grin. "I was just saying to Mr. Rupert how nice his walls would look if he had some real paintings on them instead of just plaques and stuff and that maybe you could hire an artist from your gallery for him. He laughed real loud when I said that—his face gets all wrinkly when he laughs—and then he asked me to wait a minute and brought out this sash and handed it to me! He told me this sash belonged to his mother and he wants me to have it. Should I have said no, Nan?"

"Well, it is a very fine sash indeed, and if Mr. Rupert wants you to have it, then it is a gift to be treasured. I hope you said thank you to him."

"Oh yes, I thanked Mr. Rupert. He told me this is a Métis sash, and these colours have been a part of his family for over a hundred years. That's a really long time, Nan. Look at how the colours all twist together; it's like a painting on soft strings. He told me the thicker red in the centre is called the heart of the sash. I think maybe I'll paint this on a card and give it to Mr. Rupert as a thank you. Do you think he will like that, Nan?" asks Maddy.

Nan looks down at her granddaughter and gives her a warm smile. She is pleased with Maddy's thoughtfulness and also touched by the unexpected gesture from her curmudgeonly neighbour. "Of course Mr. Rupert would love a hand-painted card from you," says Nan, kissing the top of Maddy's head. "You'd better wash your hands before dinner. Guess what we're having for dessert?"

"PIE!" holler Maddy and Nan in unison.

After dinner, Maddy sits doodling on a piece of scrap paper. "Nan, can you continue with Aggie and Mudgy while I work on my thank-you card?"

Nan lowers the weekend paper. "Okay, just wait until I finish this article and top up my peppermint tea. Remind me where we left off."

"The girls were about to leave Wrangell, but I can't remember where to. And where was Wrangell again?"

"Ah, that's right. Wrangell is in Alaska, part of the United States. Remember though, the Tlingit People have lived in this part of the world for millennia. When Aggie and Mudgy were there, the town was a busy centre where natural resources such as logging and fishing had become big industries. Many locals fished and worked in fish canneries and in the dense forests on the nearby mountains."

"And soon they were travelling on the ocean by steamship, which some people called steamers. She sailed out of Wrangell toward the port of Prince Rupert, back into Canada again, in northwestern BC.

"Aggie and Mudgy must have been bewildered, for they had never seen such large sailing vessels, nor had they ever been surrounded by crowds of people coming and going in a hurry. Not only that, but they still couldn't understand a word anyone was saying."

"Do you think the other passengers wondered why they were travelling without their parents?" asks Maddy.

"That's a good question. The other passengers might have been curious about them. Here were two little Indigenous girls in uniform with short-cropped hair, travelling alone with a priest. Perhaps an inquisitive passenger attempted to talk to them, but they were very shy and didn't speak English, so I doubt they spoke to anyone."

"How long did the voyage take?"

"They sailed for about thirteen hours from Wrangell to Prince Rupert. It was a long day of sea travel, though the scenery was and still is magnificent. Perhaps the girls stood on the ship's deck looking up at the towering coastal mountains along the route. Imagine them hanging tightly to the ship's sparkling white railing, as the vessel plied through rough sections of the Pacific Ocean.

"If they were lucky, they would have seen whales, such as orcas or migratory humpback and grey whales, surfacing and blowing tall puffs of misty air out of their blowholes. I'm sure the girls also saw seals, sea otters, and perhaps heard the roars of Steller sea lions. Marine life was so abundant back then, as were many bird species, so I bet they watched countless bald eagles circling high in the sky. Maybe they even saw some dive along the sea's surface and heard the sudden swoosh of air as the birds of prey snatched salmon with their strong, sharp talons. They might have seen puffins on rocky shores or bobbing in the ocean too. These are small birds with large orange beaks and white heads with a black ring around their necks. Very cute!

"I expect in some ways it was exciting, but it was also very distressing, for the girls knew they were so far from home now that they couldn't possibly make their own way back. The steamer sailed past many canneries approaching Prince Rupert. Salmon was ocean gold in those days. It's hard to imagine today how many fish—salmon, halibut, herring—swam in the waters. Coastal First Nations had long harvested and traded in the rich bounty of the ocean. Europeans quickly realized the value in processing fish from these waters, and over the decades they harvested so much for profit that some salmon runs are now threatened.

"The girls most likely didn't know it at the time, but Prince Rupert is a huge, deep ocean port community situated on an island—Kaien Island—that is connected to the mainland by a bridge. Many Tsimshian First Nation tribes have lived in that rugged area for millennia, and totem monuments stand tall like sentinels in their territory. The Tsimshian actively traded with other First Nations and with Europeans."

"What did they trade?"

"Before the Europeans arrived, northwestern interior and coastal First Nations traded food items such as eulachon, which is a small fish that is prized for its oil, known as eulachon grease. Maybe someday you'll get to try it. But I warn you: it has a very strong smell that might take some getting used to. I've had it on baked potatoes topped with dried seaweed, and it was yummy!

"They also traded carved horn spoons, obsidian rock, and thin little white dentalium shells. When the Europeans arrived, beaver pelts were highly sought after, as well as sea otter, mink, fox, marten, and muskrat. This became known as the fur trade, and it turned into a huge industry throughout Canada."

"Is there still a fur trade?"

"Well, yes and no—not to the degree of the original fur trade. Some First Nations trappers still trap and sell furs, and some people farm animals for their fur, but the world has changed. Fur isn't as popular as it once was, and conservation of animals is important. The poor sea otter, for example, was once on the verge of extinction due to over harvesting during the early fur trade, but thanks to conservation efforts, the sea otter is now protected and its numbers are beginning to increase."

"That's good, Nan. I like sea otters, especially when they swim with their babies on their tummies," smiles Maddy.

"I like them too," says Nan with a nod. "How's your thank-you card for Mr. Rupert coming along, Missy?"

"I'm nearly done," Maddy says, face upturned toward her Nan. "I hope he's going to like it."

Nan peers over Maddy's shoulder at the splashes of vibrant colours. "I'm sure he will. It looks a lot like the sash, so he'll have something to remember it by, which is important since it came from his family."

"Thanks, Nan. It's fun to use so many colours," Maddy says, admiring her work.

"Back to the story. When Aggie and Mudgy and the priest disembarked from the steamer, they must have looked like an odd trio. Once on shore, Father Allard leaned forward in his long, black robe and led Aggie and Mudgy in their uniforms up the steep hill to the Prince Rupert Catholic Church dormitory. Father Allard took big strides, so it wasn't easy for them to keep up with him, and the hills in Prince Rupert feel like they go almost straight up the forested mountainside.

"Anyway, they finally reached the dormitory. It was a two-storey wooden building located just down the road from the Catholic church. This would be their home for several days before they boarded a train that would take them to their final destination."

"I wonder what they thought of Prince Rupert, Nan."

"They must have been amazed at what they saw, for Prince Rupert was different from anywhere they'd been before. Wherever they went, unfamiliar sights greeted them. One unusual thing the girls probably noticed right away was that many of the sidewalks and roads—in themselves something new to them when they first set out on the journey—were built of wooden planks."

"Were the planks painted different colours?"

"No, I don't think they would have spent money on paint for the roads, but if they had, the planks would have looked beautiful in rainbow colours," replies Nan with a laugh. "Father Allard was busy with the local priest and parish, so the girls had free time to explore on their own. As Aggie and Mudgy walked along the boardwalks, they came across a wire cage with chickens pecking away at the dirt, all helter-skelter. You and I know what a chicken looks like, but the girls had only ever seen glimpses of poultry like wild grouse. Chickens were a different matter altogether.

"Somehow the girls managed to sneak under the wire into the coop and began chasing the chickens, hoping to catch one or two. They were having a great time making the chickens fly and squawk. Feathers were flying and their feet were kicking up the dirt floor something fierce, when a man came running toward them. He was shouting at the top of his lungs in a language that sounded different from anything they'd heard before, his arms flailing almost as fast as the chickens' wings were flapping.

"Aggie and Mudgy had never seen anyone who looked and dressed quite like this man, who was Chinese. His black hair was drawn tight in a thin braid down his back, and he was wearing a dark jacket with ties down the front. He was smaller than most men they had seen on their journey, but he was leaping around with so much energy, waving his arms and jumping up and down, all the while yelling in a high-pitched voice. I bet they looked at each and nodded that it was time to go. Puzzled but undeterred from further exploration, the girls quickly crawled back under the wire fence and ran down the street as fast as they could."

"That's funny, Nan. I wonder what they would have done if they had caught a chicken?" laughs Maddy.

"That would have been a fright for the chicken and a sore sight for that harried Chinese gentleman. Luckily for all, it ended peacefully, and Father Allard never found out.

"After the chicken escapade, the girls meandered along the plank sidewalk, looking this way and that when they heard an unfamiliar loud noise from behind. A black Ford Model T automobile passed by, making an unusual chugging sound. The sight and sound of the car was so different from the mail truck they had ridden in from Dease Lake to Telegraph Creek that they stood still with their mouths open for a split second and then burst into gales of laughter as the car motored past. Taking in all these new sights made the girls a bit giddy, and they couldn't stop laughing!

"Soon after, the girls came across a woman pushing an old-fashioned black pram. Its huge wheels went *click-clack* along the boardwalk. The woman was wearing a summer dress and wore a straw bonnet with a blue ribbon covering her hair.

"Being curious little beings, Aggie and Mudgy approached her, wanting to see what was inside the pram. But they didn't have the words to ask permission, so they tried gesturing with their hands. Startled by how close they were to her baby, the flustered woman purposely turned the pram away. They tried again to peer inside the carriage, but by now the woman was visibly angry and shouted, 'Go away!' Again, Aggie and Mudgy looked at each other and shrugged, walking away perplexed without ever knowing that a little baby lay sleeping inside the pram."

"That's too bad they weren't allowed to see the baby. Babies are so cute. I don't think that lady understood the girls, did she, Nan?"

"No, she didn't understand what the girls wanted. They were just curious about what was inside the pram, which was a completely foreign thing to them. It's also possible that the woman was simply uncomfortable being around First Nations people, whatever their age."

"That's weird!" Maddy says with a roll of her eyes.

"You're right, kiddo. It was an era when some people looked down upon Indigenous people as being primitive, partly because they were different from themselves.

"Before long, another amusing thing crossed their path: a man riding a dark green bicycle. The bicycle had a shiny, dome-shaped bell on its handlebars and the *ting-ting* sound coming from it entranced the girls. The rider was tall and thin, and he tapped his hat as he flew by. The girls wondered how the fellow could balance on such a thing, and of course this odd sight brought on fits of giggles. I wonder what the bicycle rider thought of a pair of giggly girls laughing at him.

"Naturally, wandering about brought on pangs of hunger. It seemed that berries played a key role on the girls' journey. As if in answer to their hunger, Aggie and Mudgy came across a huckleberry patch, and soon were gorging themselves with ripe berries. Having eaten their fill, the girls sensed it was time to head back to the dormitory. So with berry-stained hands—again—they found their way back along the boardwalk. As the girls walked into the dormitory, they were softly singing a Kaska song that Yanima had taught them while berry picking. This song served a dual purpose in that it united them as a Kaska family and also ensured that bears knew they were there.

"Their singing came to an abrupt stop when a nun noticed their dirty hands. 'Go wash your hands NOW!' she yelled, pointing her finger to the washroom down the hallway. They hung their heads and walked as quickly as they could, and without even thinking, the girls ran their berry-stained hands along the pristine white walls. The shiny walls were so different from their small log cabin that only a sense of touch could help them understand. The smoothness of the walls felt cool on their hands.

"The washroom faucets also caused them some confusion. They figured out how to turn the faucets on but not how to turn them off. Not knowing what else to do, they simply left the room. Of course, water was soon pouring all over the floor, causing a minor flood. Someone noticed the flooding water and the berry stains, so the nuns made Aggie and Mudgy clean the walls. They set to work with a bucket of hot, soapy water, but no matter how hard they scrubbed, the stains only faded a little. The nuns probably knew all along that the dormitory walls would only recover with a fresh coat of paint."

"I hope they weren't scolded too much. After all, they didn't know the berries would stain the walls."

"I hope they weren't too. A lot of changes were happening quickly to Aggie and Mudgy and even more changes were on the way. They must have fallen into bed with many unanswered questions whirling around in their heads. With no one to comfort them or to explain what was happening, I imagine they were two very anxious young girls. But at least they had each other.

"Now, Missy, it is getting late," Nan growls with a mock-serious voice. "Time for bed for you too. Tomorrow is another day for more storytelling. Go get your PJs on."

NAN HAS a fitful sleep. She can never fall asleep easily knowing that a member of the household is still out. When she hears her daughter's car pull into the driveway just after midnight, she finally relaxes and drifts off. Her sleep is interspersed with dreams.

One dream haunts Nan. She sees a small dark-haired girl in a lemony-yellow dress playing on the banks of a river; the river is high and moving fast. The little girl is picking up river stones, unaware of the hazard nearby. Desperately, Nan tries to reach her, to warn her of the imminent danger. Swirling water is surging right beside the little girl.

It's as though a heat shield prevents her from grasping the girl. Nan senses that this little person is deeply cherished. The child's identity is unclear, as well as her fate beside the menacing river. Nan awakes with her heart pounding and notices the bed sheets are damp with sweat. She lies still for a long time before sleep returns.

## CHAPTER SEVEN
# Brunch and Dahlias

THE FOLLOWING morning, Nan rises early to begin breakfast preparations. Sunday is the day of decadent breakfasts. Maddy is a fan of pancakes, so Nan uses the leftover Spartan apples and makes apple batter pancakes. She brushes rashers of bacon with maple syrup and pops them into the oven. Fresh blueberries and yogurt are also on the breakfast menu. Lucas knows that Sunday is a good day to drop by early, so it's not surprising that Buskers' tail begins to whip back and forth as Lucas peers through the backdoor window. Nan laughs and lets him in.

"Hey, Lucas! You're just in time for some breakfast," says Nan with a welcoming smile, "Unless of course you aren't hungry."

"Well, if it's okay with you, it's okay with me," grins Lucas as he scratches Buskers' ears. He quickly sits down beside Maddy and surveys the breakfast table with delight. Lucas rewards the family by sharing highlights from the previous night's Canucks hockey game. Lucas is a huge hockey fan. Buskers plants himself on the floor between Maddy and Lucas, hoping some delectable tidbit falls to the floor.

The small family and guest feast contentedly upon their Sunday morning breakfast. Nan suggests that Lucas finish the last pancake—which he heartedly agrees to—and afterward he is permitted to reward Buskers with one reserved slice of maple bacon.

Cherrie notices dark circles under her mother's eyes. She chides herself for staying out later than usual last evening. "Mom, that was a delicious breakfast. Thank you," she says. "I'll take Maddy and Lucas—if he is allowed to and wants to join us—to Jericho Beach today. Buskers can come along as well."

"Sounds like a wonderful plan," says Nan savouring the idea of solitary time. "Don't forget to take some snacks with you. I'll catch up on some of my writing while you hunt for treasures on the beach."

As Nan settles down with her laptop, she notices Mr. Rupert outside watering his dahlias. He putters outside less and less now. He employs an ancient gardener and handyman about twice a month; Mr. Rupert is likely one of his few remaining clients. Nan smiles as she thinks of the two crotchety old guys fussing and tenderly caring for Mr. Rupert's dahlias. Immersed in her work, Nan doesn't hear the knock on the backdoor. A louder knock gets her attention. Mr. Rupert is standing in the doorway, holding an immense armload of multi-coloured dahlias.

"Here, these are for you," Mr. Rupert says gruffly, shoving the bouquet toward Nan. "I just want to say thank you for all the pies and muffins over the years. You… no, I mean you and your family are fine neighbours and I appreciate your kindness. Rupert Lane is fortunate to have you and that's all I have to say about it."

Nan is taken aback by Mr. Rupert's gesture, but she smiles and pulls the bouquet to her nose. "Why, these are beautiful, Mr. Rupert. Thank you very much. Um, would you like to come in for a cup of tea?"

"No, sorry. I don't have time for tea today. I just wanted you to have the dahlias, that's all," growls Mr. Rupert as he turns on his cane and hobbles back toward his house. "And thank that talented granddaughter of yours for her wee art card. It wouldn't be out of place hanging in the Queen's gallery!"

## CHAPTER EIGHT

# Train Travel Inland

THE FOLLOWING weekend, Lucas and Maddy's time outdoors comes to a halt when the skies open up with a typical autumn downpour. Peeling off wet yellow anoraks and boots, the pair hovers around Nan, hoping that she will carry on with Aggie and Mudgy. Nan takes the hint and nestles into her favourite green chair. Maddy and Lucas plop down on the floor with their backs against the couch. Nan begins: "I believe we left the girls in Prince Rupert cleaning berry stains off dormitory walls, and they were just about to embark on the next leg of their journey—boarding a train.

"It was now approaching mid-August, and early one morning, Aggie and Mudgy were wakened by a nun who hurriedly motioned to them to get dressed. After a small breakfast, Father Allard came to collect them.

"The trio walked along 5th Avenue and gradually headed down the sloping boardwalks toward the ocean. The views were magnificent with the morning summer sun reflecting off the sea; however, the girls had learned it was best to be silent while near the priest, so they resisted the temptation to comment on the scenery or chat about where they might be going next.

"Soon they saw a red brick building perched along the waterfront. This was the Prince Rupert railway station. There were folks with bags waiting nearby and workers hustling to and fro. Long iron tracks seemed to stretch out forever. Here, the priest and the girls would board the train, leaving Prince Rupert and the ocean far behind."

"Had Aggie and Mudgy ever travelled on a train before?" asks Lucas. "I haven't, but I'd sure like to."

"Actually, it was the first time they had ever *seen* a train. It must have seemed like a giant iron carriage to them, don't you think? The whistles were loud, the steam from the engines puffed giant clouds into the air, and the passenger cars rocked back and forth along the tracks.

"On board, the priest pointed to a set of seats facing each other, and Aggie and Mudgy sat closely together opposite Father Allard. He took out papers from his case and began reading. As he was occupied, the girls pressed their faces against the window.

"The train slowly chugged out of the station and through the town. Then it passed through thick groves of cedar trees and then through the coastal mountains. Cascading waterfalls occasionally interrupted thick green mountain slopes. These were exciting to spy!

"It wasn't long before the train tracks began to follow a large waterway—the mighty Skeena River. Like other northern river systems, the Skeena River has long sustained Indigenous communities along its route, namely the Gitxsan, Wet'suwet'en, and Tsimshian First Nations. Its name is derived from the Gitxsan word 'Ksan, meaning 'River of the Mists.'

"Aggie and Mudgy likely saw fleets of commercial gillnetters drifting their way through the vast river currents. Fishers could be seen harvesting huge nets of Coho salmon on the river as the girls sped down the tracks in their rocking railcar.

"With their noses to the window, the girls whispered quietly to each other. Aggie sensed Mudgy's anxiety about their future and tried to think of ways to distract her. She remembered a story that Yanima used to tell called 'The Sisters Who Married Stars.' She didn't fully understand the tale, but she always listened attentively when Yanima spoke.

"The priest had nodded off in his seat, so the girls were free to speak to each other in Kaska. Aggie spoke in a low voice: 'Listen, Mudgy. I'm going to tell you a story that comes from Yanima. I want you to try to remember this story.'

"Mudgy nodded her head and said quietly, 'Okay, I'll try to remember.'

"'Once, two sisters made camp together and looked up high in the night sky,' Aggie began. 'They saw many brilliant stars. Two of the stars stood out amongst the rest, one dazzling white star and one dazzling red star. One sister said to the other, *I shall take that red star for my husband, and you may take the white star for your husband.* That night when asleep, they went up to the stars and lived with them as husband and wife. Their star husbands were excellent hunters, and they never went hungry. Though their bellies were always full, and they wanted for nothing, the sisters missed their Earth family. They decided to try to come back to Earth.

" 'They cut up skins and made a long, long rope. One day when their husbands were away hunting, they slid down the rope and eventually reached Earth. Trying to find their way back to their village, the sisters encountered Wolverine near the river. Wolverine was dishonest and tricky. He wanted to keep the sisters for himself. The sisters told Wolverine that he must go hunting and bring back caribou meat for them. While he was gone, the sisters hurried to the river crossing, where they met a river snipe.

" 'The snipe had a long bill and could transform itself into a ferry that crossed the river. They asked the river snipe to drown Wolverine while ferrying him across the river. The snipe agreed only after the sisters guaranteed to pay him with porcupine quills, so the sisters gave all of their porcupine quills to the snipe. Wolverine tracked the sisters to the river and demanded that the snipe carry him across. The snipe kept his word and drowned Wolverine.

" 'Later, after they crossed the river, the sisters knew they were close to their village and parents. After their reunion, they asked their father to build a bridge for them whenever they were near water. Their father always did, except one time he neglected to build a small bridge over a young creek. The two sisters vanished and never came back. Their mother searched and searched for them. One day while searching, the mother saw two beavers in a stream where they had built a house. She knew these were her daughters and that they would always be beavers swimming in the stream.'

"'Do you think Yanima will search for us, Aggie?' whispered Mudgy.

"'She will always keep a watch for our return,' Aggie said carefully, turning her face away to hide her sorrow.

"The train meandered along its tracks following the Skeena River for what seemed a very long time to the girls, though it was only about three hours at that point. Eventually the train slowed and made its first stop in the small town of Terrace.

"In those days, Terrace was a forestry town that milled and transported timber worldwide. When the train approached Terrace, Aggie and Mudgy saw a small, hut-like building. It was the train station where passengers purchased tickets and waited inside on wooden benches prior to boarding. Beyond the station, some wooden buildings and homes dotted the landscape farther from the tracks. I don't think the girls left the train, for it only stopped long enough for people to get on and off before the porter yelled, 'All aboard! All aboard!' in a loud voice."

"I bet they got hungry on board the train. I wonder if they had anything to eat?" asks Maddy, looking at Nan and Lucas.

"Yeah, I'd be starving!" says Lucas nodding his head.

"You're right! I imagine they did get hungry and thirsty," replies Nan. "I suspect that the nuns from the church in Prince Rupert provided some food for their journey. Maybe they ate some cheese or bologna sandwiches, something easy to pack."

"Hey, bologna sandwiches sounds scrumpdillyicious!" says Lucas, rubbing his belly.

"We'll see if we can add some bologna to our Sunday brunch," replies Nan with a smile.

"Now, after leaving Terrace, the train tracks continued alongside the Skeena River for many miles until they reached the next destination—the little town of Hazelton. Hazelton sits at the junction of the Skeena and Bulkley Rivers and a mountain named Stegyawden towers over the town. It is believed that ancient chiefs travelled great distances to meet at the base of Stegyawden. Many First Nations people regard it as a sacred mountain. Stegyawden comes from a Tsimshian name meaning 'painted goat.'"

"Do you think Aggie and Mudgy were allowed off the train to see the mountain?" asks Maddy.

"You know, I think it's quite possible that they did, for this was close to the mid-point of their train journey, and they needed to stretch their legs. As they got off the train, they saw a small railway station. Big wagons were waiting for baggage and freight to be unloaded from the train. Near the tracks, the small town of mostly wooden houses and a few stores spread out. The Bulkley River flowed on the other side of the tracks. The roads were dirt and the sidewalks were made of elevated wooden boards. Hazelton was a very young town, only about sixty years old then. It has grown considerably since.

"Maybe one day you'll travel to Hazelton yourselves. It's currently home to the 'Ksan Historical Village and Museum, so I think you'd like it. Visitors can witness the culture and art of the local Indigenous Peoples. Many First Nations artists continue to apprentice at 'Ksan under master carvers and artists. Depending on the time of year, you're likely to see artists demonstrating their skills. It's amazing how creative and dedicated to their craft they are!

"Maddy, remember seeing the giant forest paintings at the Vancouver Art Gallery by Emily Carr? You liked her tall swirling trees. Well, Emily Carr also painted in Hazelton. The National Gallery of Canada has *Totem Pole at Hazelton*, painted by Carr in 1912, so she was likely in the Hazelton area less than twenty years before the girls passed through."

"Oh, yes," replies Maddy enthusiastically. "I remember Emily Carr's giant swirling trees. It's like they are moving, almost dancing, in the wind. I can show Lucas some of her paintings later."

"Yes, and show Lucas an image of *Totem Pole at Hazelton*. If I remember correctly, Miss Carr included Stegyawden in her little masterpiece. You'll see a glimpse of historic Hazelton and that majestic mountain."

"Hey, Maddy," Lucas says with a sly grin. "One day I'm gonna see one of *your* paintings in a gallery. Hmmm... I think you'd better start working on more paintings of ME!"

Maddy rolls her eyes and playfully slugs Lucas on the arm. "Sure thing, Mr. Artsy Model. Better work on your poses!" Despite the jesting, Maddy was secretly pleased at Lucas' comment.

"You never know what the future will bring," said Nan, acknowledging the pleasure in Maddy's face, before turning back to the story.

"Okay, now. Having re-boarded the train, the girls watched as it continued to follow a winding river, but it wasn't the Skeena. They left the Skeena River behind at Hazelton, and now the train followed the Bulkley River, heading toward the town of Smithers. The Bulkley River is not as massive as the Skeena, but it is a considerable size and is also well known for salmon fishing. Halfway between Hazelton and Smithers is the small community of Witset, formerly known as Moricetown. Witset's original Wet'suwet'en name was Kyah Wiget, which means 'old village.' Witset translates into 'the people of the first village.' Nearby, Witset Canyon is a dramatic waterway famous for traditional fishing."

"How come this place had so many names?" asks a puzzled Lucas.

"Excellent question, Lucas. Maddy and I talked about this before, so I'm glad you asked.

Indigenous Peoples didn't change their place names. They were changed without their consent. When European settlers began arriving, they couldn't speak or understand Indigenous languages. They presumed that English was better for everyone and gave traditional villages, rivers, mountains, and valleys English names. It was one of many ways that they started to take possession of lands that weren't really theirs to take. Think about it. When we name something, it gives us a kind of ownership, doesn't it? Witset is a very recent example of Indigenous Peoples taking back ownership of their languages and returning to their traditional place names."

"Wow, that's kinda cool, being able to change names. If I had a choice I'd change my name to Sir Lucas and make my stupid brother bow to me. But I guess that's not really what we're talking about here."

"Duh, you think, Sir Lucas?" laughs Maddy.

Nan chuckles at the thought of Lucas becoming knighted.

"Just think about where we live. The city of Vancouver and Vancouver Island were named after British captain George Vancouver, who sailed into this area in the 1790s, but if you research this area's history, you will find that Vancouver was and still is home to Coast Salish Peoples—the Musqueam, Squamish and Tsleil-Waututh Nations—who had long identified their place names in their own languages.

"I'll give you one example that I know both of you are very familiar with—Stanley Park. Stanley Park was named after Lord Frederick Stanley, who was Governor General of Canada when the park opened in 1888. I am sure we have walked by Lord Stanley's statue in the centre of the park many times. Anyway, prior to the creation of Stanley Park, this area was known as X̱wáy̓x̱way, a name that means 'ancient masked dance.' You pronounce it like *Kwhy-kway*—give it a try."

"*Kwhy-kway…Kwhy-kway,*" sputter Maddy and Lucas.

"That's it," says Nan smiling. "The next time we visit Stanley Park, think about the many ancient peoples who lived, fished, and gathered seafood at X̱wáýx̱way. They were the first caretakers of that precious space."

"They took really good care of X̱wáýx̱way 'cause it's still amazing and one of my favourite spots," says Maddy.

"Mine too!" nods Lucas.

"Okay, back to the train journey. The train was passing through Witset on its way to Smithers. The town of Smithers is in the Bulkley Valley and surrounded by mountains, namely the Babine Range and Hudson Bay Mountain. It is very picturesque. Today, many people ski at Smithers and enjoy all sorts of outdoor recreation, but when Aggie and Mudgy travelled through it was a much smaller mill town. It's likely that the train made a stop at Smithers to pick up or drop off passengers.

"As the train rambled out of Smithers, the girls huddled together. They had no idea how long they were going to be on the train. Or where their final destination would be. When the priest left the railcar to speak to the train conductor, the girls quickly spoke to each other in their native tongue.

"'How far do we ride on this rocking horse?' asked a worried Mudgy. 'Where will we sleep tonight, Aggie?

Do we sleep on these seats? Do you have anything left to eat?'

"'Maybe we do. We can lie together to keep warm. Maybe the priest has more food for us to eat. When we see our brothers again, we can tell them about the boats, the mail truck, and the train. They probably would like to see the things that we have seen. Maybe this new school will be a fine school, and we will tell Yanima that we are good girls. She will be happy if we are good at school. Let's look outside again and search for animals. Maybe moose or caribou are nearby, maybe eagles are fishing, maybe...'

"'NO KASKA—SPEAK ENGLISH!' shouted Father Allard, who had come back to his seat across from the girls.

"Aggie and Mudgy froze and stared stonily ahead. The priest glared at them and then resumed his reading. Somehow the girls knew that the train tracks were taking them farther and farther from their home. They were lost in a void, not understanding where they would end up. School was one of the English words that they knew; however, they deeply wished school was a place closer to home. This sounds unimaginable, but that's what happened to Aggie and Mudgy and countless other children like them."

Nan notices that Lucas has a troubled look on his face. "Imagine if you were told that as of tomorrow you could no longer speak English," she said. "What would you do?"

"I dunno what I'd do," Lucas replies. "Guess I'd try to learn as much as I could about the language I was supposed to be speaking, but I'd want to talk to Maddy in English for sure. How else could we talk about what was going on?"

"You know, I think that might be exactly how Aggie and Mudgy felt. It sure raises an awful lot of questions about our lives and our ancestors' lives, doesn't it? Sometimes it's good to ask questions even if they sound silly."

Maddy is sitting still, listening intently, and Lucas is fidgeting beside her.

"You seem restless, Lucas," Nan says. "Should we take a break?"

He pauses and then blurts out, "My stepmom says that your telling of Aggie and Mudgy doesn't make sense and that you are just making things up. She says that too many stories get exaggerated in order to make them seem bigger and that the past is the past. Sometimes I just don't know what to think!"

Nan looks fondly at her young red-headed neighbour and inhales deeply.

She slowly formulates her words. "I'm sorry that your stepmom thinks that way, Lucas. Many people do. But I want you both to understand something: the journey of Aggie and Mudgy is a true story. Truth comes from many sources, and sometimes these sources appear in surprising forms. In your school, you look up information through your textbooks, libraries, and the internet, but there are also different ways of discovering information.

"There are stories and legends passed down through generations in something we call oral history. Long before people learned to write, civilizations taught life lessons and their histories to upcoming generations through stories. Many of these stories are still taught in Indigenous communities and by Indigenous people, and they aren't anything like what you read in your history textbooks today.

"Think about monuments carved in wood and stone, underground middens, family histories stitched onto clothing and weavings, paintings, dance, and song. All of these contribute to learning truths about people and places. Aggie and Mudgy's story doesn't belong to me, or Maddy, or you, Lucas; it originates from the Kaska people. This story is Kaska history and, as such, is now part of Canada's history as well. Do you understand what I'm trying to say?"

"I think so," says Lucas in a small voice. "Maybe my stepmom needs a cup of tea with you, Nan."

Nan permits herself a small smile and suggests it's time for a snack.

AFTER PUTTING the fruit, cheese, and crackers away, Nan carefully places her Darjeeling tea on the coaster and begins her tale anew.

"Okay, now that everyone is sufficiently refuelled, let's carry on. The train left Smithers and was heading toward the little communities of Telkwa and Houston. Both of these communities are located in the Bulkley Valley, which is good ranch and farmland.

"Each train station they passed had the name of the community printed in large black letters hanging on a sign, though of course at that time Aggie and Mudgy couldn't understand what the dark markings on the signs meant. The train slowly passed through Telkwa and on toward Houston. The girls had been travelling on the train for close to eight long hours at this point.

"With a short stop in Houston, the girls noticed a log cabin directly across from the railway station, and they probably saw the postmistress who ran the Houston post office for many years. I imagine she was a resource-ful woman who knew all the railway workers by name and everyone who lived in Houston. I can picture her dressed in a floor-length flowered skirt and apron, standing in the doorway waiting to exchange mailbags with the train conductor. She likely saw two little dark-haired girls peering out the train window and waved them farewell as the train pulled out of the station."

"Cool, a log cabin. I'd like to have a job there," says Lucas wistfully.

"Yeah, I wish we had a log cabin," echoes Maddy.

"They make fine homes, just like the log home where Aggie and Mudgy lived, in Daylu." Nan says. "Soon after leaving Houston, the girls noticed that the river had disappeared. For the first time since leaving Prince Rupert they were not following a river anymore. The scenic river was replaced with large forests of pine, spruce, and birch trees. They were now in lake country and heading toward the town of Burns Lake, which you may have guessed is located beside a lake named Burns Lake.

"When Europeans first settled this community, forest fires had ravaged the area, so they named it Burnt Lake, which later morphed into Burns Lake. After leaving the little community, the train moved toward its final stop for the travelling trio. The last flag stop the train rolled through was Endako, a tiny community situated a mere thirteen kilometres from their final destination at Fraser Lake.

"Of course, the girls didn't know they were getting close to the end of their journey. They had no idea of the distance they had travelled that day. They only knew that they were travelling farther and farther away from home."

Nan ceases her narrative as she reflects upon how thirteen kilometres led to a terrible destination for Aggie and Mudgy. She stretches her arms out and states: "That's enough story for today, you two. I think Buskers and I need a walk."

CHAPTER NINE

# Arrival at Lejac Residential School

THE FOLLOWING Sunday evening, Nan has just sat down with her tea and is about to open her favourite art magazine when her granddaughter plops down beside her and asks if she would carry on with the story. Cherrie is nearby at the kitchen table, immersed in marking papers. Nan slides her magazine to one side, knowing that she could savour it after Maddy's bedtime. Smiling at her young face, Nan simply says: "Of course, where were we?"

"I think the girls were nearing the end of their journey," says Maddy. "And don't worry about Lucas. I told him I'd tell him the rest tomorrow."

"Okay. Yes, you're right. Aggie and Mudgy were approaching the end of their train journey. Can you guess how far they had travelled from their home in Daylu?"

"Ummm … maybe six hundred kilometres?" Maddy asks.

"Nope, your guess is too low. I'll try to break it down for you a little bit. First, they travelled by riverboat from Daylu to Dease Lake, which was about 320 kilometres. Their mail truck drive from Dease Lake to Telegraph Creek was 116 kilometres. Telegraph Creek to Wrangell via paddlewheeler boat was 257 kilometres. Steamship travel from Wrangell, Alaska, to Prince Rupert was close to 350 kilometres. Train travel from Prince Rupert to Fraser Lake, 563 kilometres. So, the total distance the girls had travelled was 1,609 kilometres!"

"Wow, that's a mega journey! How many days were they travelling again, Nan?"

"They left Daylu early in July 1928. They arrived at Fraser Lake in mid-August, so including several stays along the way, they were travelling for close to six weeks."

"That's a really long time away. I know I'd be home-sick for you and Mommy and Buskers!" says Maddy seriously.

"Missy, you would be severely missed by many folks AND by a certain dog!" says Nan as she pats Maddy's nose with her finger.

"Okay, back to the train. The train left the little stop of Endako and pushed onward. The terrain was flat without noticeable landmarks. After several miles, a small body of water came into view, followed by a much larger one. This was Fraser Lake, a very large lake almost twenty kilometres long. Fraser Lake is known as Nadleh Bun by the local Dakelh First Nations. Nadleh refers to where the salmon return every year. Nadleh Bun is home to both the Nadleh Whut'en, on the east side of the lake, and the Stellat'en First Nation, on the west side.

"The train rambled along the tracks following the edge of the lake. I imagine the girls were tired from their long journey, but they must have peered out at the large body of water in wonder. It was still summer, the days were long, and as the sun shone on the lake I bet they wished they could spend the afternoon splashing in the cool blue water."

"Maybe they would have enjoyed a picnic by the lake too, Nan," muses Maddy.

"Why, yes. I'm sure the girls would have loved a picnic," Nan says, "but the school wasn't exactly a picnic type of school." Nan catches Cherrie rolling her eyes at this comment.

"That's too bad," Maddy says matter-of-factly.

"Several kilometres down the track, the girls sensed a change. The wheels of the train were slowing, and the priest began gathering his belongings. Father Allard had an impatient air about him, as though he was soon to be released from an unpleasant yet charitable mission. He snapped his fingers at Aggie and Mudgy and motioned for them to follow him to the railcar door. The train chugged to a slow grinding crawl. Just beyond the curve of the lake was a tiny railway station hut with black markings that spelled L-E-J-A-C."

"This was their new school, right, Nan?" asks Maddy.

"Yes, this was their new school," replies Nan in a soft voice.

"Their school wasn't like my school, was it, Nan?"

"No, Maddy. It was nothing like your school," replies Nan, a faraway look in her eyes.

Cherrie listens carefully to her mother's words. This is a familiar tale to her ears but a very new tale for her daughter. She resists an urge to gently cover her daughter's ears with her hands and place little kisses on her forehead.

"Mom, do you want to take a break?" asks Cherrie. "Maddy can hear the rest another day."

"No, I think we're good for a bit longer," says Nan, giving her daughter a reassuring glance. "Now, when the girls and Father Allard stepped down from the railway car, they were the only figures left standing by the side of the tracks—one tall man clad all in black and two little girls in matching dark grey uniforms, holding hands. "Aggie and Mudgy looked apprehensively up the sloping grassy hill. In the distance, they could see a large, square brick building. It looked cold even in the warmth of a summer day. The front of the building faced the train tracks along Fraser Lake, while the back entrance faced the road.

"In time, Aggie and Mudgy came to know the surrounding buildings and grounds of Lejac intimately, but on that day long ago, as their small legs tried to keep up with the priest walking up the hill, they did not notice the lagoon to the right, the barn in the field, the church behind the school, or the small graveyard to their left."

"Were other children outside, Nan?" asks Maddy.

"Well, there may have been. Even though it was summer, many children couldn't go home to their families."

"That's not good," says Maddy with a frown.

"You're right. It wasn't very good at all, but that's the way it was for some. Aggie and Mudgy shuffled their ugly brown Oxfords up the hill silently for five long minutes, and as they got closer, all they could see were four storeys of red brick with two wings on each side. Four rows of windows stared out at them, and a wide wooden stairway led to a front door.

"Mudgy clasped her sister's hand tighter as Father Allard pushed open the door. Aggie and Mudgy crossed the threshold into a building that would be their home for the next ten years. Black cloth surrounded the girls as the dark robes of several nuns enveloped them and suffocated the air. The large front door thudded loudly, shutting out the sunshine."

"Nan, your voice sounds froggy. Do you want some more tea?" asks Maddy.

"No thanks, dear, but maybe I am a bit tired. Perhaps we'll carry on later," says Nan, her voice suddenly drained.

"Come on, Maddy. Time to hop in the bath," calls Cherrie. "School day tomorrow for both of us, kiddo."

After leaving Maddy surrounded by books on her bed following her bath, Cherrie walks back to the kitchen. Her mother remains sitting still in her chair, absently scratching Buskers' ears. Cherrie puts the kettle on and places some shortbread on a plate for the two of them. She wishes she could soothe the sorrow reflected in her mother's dark brown eyes. She waits quietly.

Nan breaks the silence and speaks in a low, restrained voice: "I am a coward, and I'm weak. I just can't utter the words to my granddaughter. I am so sorry, Cherrie. I'm not being fair leaving it to you to finish the tale. I simply can't express to Maddy what they went through at Lejac. You were right. She's too young.

"How can I explain children suffering, forced from the safety and love of family to end up isolated, lonely, and scared? How do I explain that Aggie and Mudgy suffered even more isolation because, unlike most other students, they were desperately far from their community, spoke a distinct language, and had different customs and features?

"How can I tell her that their only source of protein for ten years was beef fat spread on a slice of bread, except for Easter morning when they each received one boiled egg? How can anyone make sense of the shrill whistle that demanded their daily and hourly attention? The whistle began early. All students awoke at 6:00 in the morning and made their beds. By 6:30, they lined up for morning church. At 7:00 a.m., they lined up for breakfast. At 8:15, the girls began their household chores, sweeping, dusting, and washing. The boys worked outside as unpaid labourers, milking cows, tending to the chickens, weeding, and harvesting vegetables. The 9:00 a.m. whistle was a call to go to class. The 11:30 whistle meant lining up for lunch. By 1:30 in the afternoon, the whistle called them to go back to class. The 4:30 whistle called the children to line up for supper. The 6:30

whistle was a call to line up for church. Finally, the 8:00 p.m. whistle called the children to line up to go to their dormitories, silence strictly enforced within the cold, dark, bare rooms.

"And how can I possibly talk about the physical and mental cruelty that grown men and women forced onto the children? Or account for the small graves, hidden or not, of little souls who died in their midst, far away from home—dead from tuberculosis, neglect, and broken spirits?"

Cherrie squeezes her mother's hand as they both look out into the fading light of the evening sky.

# CHAPTER TEN
# Maddy's Gift
# to Nan

THE FOLLOWING WEEKS hum with activity. Christmas is approaching rapidly, one of Nan's favourite holidays. Rupert Lane is bright with festive lights hung on houses, trees, and bushes. Walking Buskers is a joy as homes glow with seasonal sparkle. Nan loves seeing the twinkle of lit-up Christmas trees through windows. Even Mr. Rupert has his handyman up on a ladder putting up ancient multi-coloured bulbs from the 1950s. Nan laughs to herself as she thinks of Mr. Rupert and his now-trendy collection of vintage Christmas decorations.

She loves the crispness in the air and secretly wishes for a dusting of snow, something that rarely falls in their coastal climate. Nan loves Christmas carols—even the corny ones—and sings without fear of others hearing her. Most of all, Nan loves watching her granddaughter at this festive time of year. She is content watching Maddy laughing with Cherrie and herself as they bake special goodies, make homemade cards, and whisper about secret gift exchanges.

Nan knows that her own early Christmases had a deep influence on her outlook. With four much older brothers and sisters, it was as though she had six parents to indulge her. Despite twinges in her bones and occasional loneliness, Nan feels exceedingly blessed.

"Well, that's the last present to be wrapped. HO-HO-HO, Mom," quips Cherrie as she adds several more logs onto the smouldering fire.

"The tree looks fantastic! You and Maddy did a great job decorating this year. How did it get to be Christmas Eve already? December drains away far too quickly! Where is our girl? I thought she would be down shaking some of the presents under the tree."

"She has some last-minute wrapping to do—a special present for a special someone," says Cherrie with a grin.

"Ooooh . . . it must be for her mom. By the way," Nan drops her voice so Maddy can't overhear, "has her father sent her something this year?"

"Noooo, this special present isn't for me, and yes, thank God he did send her something for Christmas. He's going to call Maddy on Skype tomorrow morning. At least he's putting some effort into maintaining a relationship with her," sighs Cherrie.

Before Nan can reply, Buskers' toenails click down the hallway floor. They know that Maddy is likely right behind him, so they quickly change the subject from absent father to Father Christmas.

"I heard on the CBC news that there have been some strange sightings in the sky this evening," says Nan with a grin.

"You're right, Mom. I heard that as well. I wonder what's going on?" replies Cherrie.

"Ooooh ... you guys!" says Maddy in a serious eight-year-old voice. "You can't fool me about flying sleighs. I am much too old for that one!"

Nan and Cherrie feign surprised looks, watching in amusement as Maddy sneaks a quick look out into the dark sky. Maddy has a wrapped present tucked under her arm, festooned with bows and ribbons and multi-coloured stickers. She is proud of her wrapping and carefully places the package under the tree.

"Nan, do you like my wrapping job?" asks Maddy, admiring the gift.

"Why, it's glitteringly lovely, my dear," Nan says with outstretched arms. "Here, come give me a hug! I can tell you put a lot of thought into this one, my girl."

"I'm glad you like it, Nan. I can't wait until you open it."

"It's something to look forward to," says Nan with a smile.

"Nan, I have a question I've been wanting to ask, but it's Christmas Eve and I don't want you to be sad."

"Well, my pet, this sounds like an important question, and important questions need to be asked and answered. Fire away."

Maddy takes a deep breath. "Nan, I've really enjoyed your story about Aggie and Mudgy, even though some of it makes you sad. But I don't understand how you know so much about them when you never met them. Who were they really?"

For the next few moments, the house is silent. The only sounds are the crackling flames burning in the fireplace.

Maddy watches her grandmother closely.

Cherrie watches both her mother and daughter.

Nan places her arm around her granddaughter and plants a kiss on top of her head. She has anticipated this question for a long time, and tonight words will not fail her. Patting Maddy on the knee, Nan rises to her feet, reaches toward the desk drawer, and finds the faded photograph of Aggie and Mudgy. Standing near the fireplace, Nan looks at the photograph by the light of the fire. She sees two little girls standing close to each other. Both of them stare straight ahead at the photographer without smiling. Nan's breathing is now relaxed. Her head feels clear and light. Nan looks over at her daughter and granddaughter and smiles.

"This old photograph is the only thing that I have of Aggie and Mudgy," Nan says, returning to her chair and beckoning Maddy to join her. "It's not worth much, but it is invaluable to me. You have a right to know who these two girls were. Look carefully into their faces, Maddy. What do you see?"

Maddy peers intently into their faces and then studies Nan's face. "I think maybe they belong to us somehow," she says tentatively.

"You are absolutely right, Maddy. The taller girl on the left is your great-great-auntie Aggie, and the shorter girl on the right is your great-grandmother Mudgy. Mudgy was my birth mother. When I was born, Mudgy wasn't able to keep me for many reasons, so I was adopted into a loving family who raised me. I never met Aggie and

Mudgy because they both passed on before I was old enough to find them. So, my dear, their story is a part of who we are, and we need to always remember that."

Cherrie watches as her daughter quietly crawls out of her grandmother's arms and fetches her carefully wrapped gift from under the tree. Maddy stands in front of her grandmother and places the gift on her lap. Maddy clasps Nan's hands and whispers something into her ear.

Overwhelmed with emotion, Cherrie observes her mom and daughter while remaining rooted in her chair. She resists a strong urge to gather Maddy in her arms, yet she doesn't want to interrupt the magic unfolding between her mother and daughter. But her eyes are moist, and she is bursting with pride and love.

Nan slowly opens her gift. Inside the decorated paper is a painting. Nan gasps in delight. It is an image of Aggie and Mudgy painted in a warm radiance of yellows, gold, and amber.

"Do you like it, Nan?" Maddy asks in a little voice.

"Like it? I absolutely love it, Maddy!" Nan exclaims.

Maddy beams. "Mom helped me scan the photograph, and then we mounted it on a canvas and painted it with acrylics."

Cherrie leans over her mother's shoulder and inspects Maddy's painting.

"You've taught her colours so well, Mom," Cherrie says, pointing to the deep sapphire blue of the outer perimeter. "Look how she painted all of us around Aggie and Mudgy."

"Yes, indeed!" Nan holds the painting with outstretched arms to admire the composition of family and neighbours, including Nan, Cherrie, Maddy and her father, Buskers, Lucas, and even Mr. Rupert. In between, the canvas is filled with the moon, sun, constellations, rivers, forests, mountains, waterfalls, rainbows, exquisite flowers, feathers, fish, baskets, and hearts. It is a visual cornucopia of delights.

Maddy watches Nan place her gift on the mantle. She reaches for her mother's hand, and the three of them stand together, admiring the painting in its place of prominence. The room radiates luminous warmth, with Aggie and Mudgy right in the centre.

The small family inside 113 Rupert Lane glows with tenderness and love. Outside, smoke from the chimney seems to dance its way high into the heavens.

THE END

# Epilogue

LEAVING LEJAC Residential School in the late 1930s, Aggie and Mudgy found employment as domestic workers in separate households. They eventually ended up in the Prince George area of British Columbia. Aggie married a European man and had five children. The marriage was not a happy one. Mudgy found some contentment with her first common-law relationship. After the death of this man, she entered into a long-term relationship that was fraught with difficulties and abuse. She never married. Mudgy gave birth to twelve children. Eight of her children were placed into the care of social services at birth, with some remaining as permanent foster-care children and some adopted. I was one of these eight, who was adopted as an infant into a non-Indigenous family.

While still a student at Lejac, Mudgy returned once to her home in Daylu (Lower Post) and saw her mother Yanima just before she passed. She never returned to her place of birth again.

After leaving Lejac, Aggie returned for one visit to Daylu. Aggie died in 2001 and is buried in the Elders' cemetery across the Liard River in Daylu. Mudgy died in 1976 and is buried in the Prince George City cemetery.

Father Elphège Allard, Oblats de Marie-Immaculée, continued removing Indigenous children from their homes to residential schools until 1935. On July 13, 1935, Father Allard was travelling with another priest to Daylu along the Dease River when their outboard motor quit. As Allard stood up to turn in order to look at the motor, the unguided boat drifted along the current around a bend where a mature tree extended over the water. The tree hit Allard hard and knocked him into the Dease River. The other priest managed to get ashore and find help while walking along the Davies Grease Trail. The RCMP eventually found Allard's body snagged to a root along the riverbank.

Lejac Residential School closed in 1976. The school buildings were eventually razed, and the land was transferred to the local Nadleh Whut'en First Nation. The Rose Prince Memorial and the small cemetery are all that remain on the former residential school site.

I grew up in Prince George, BC, but have lived in Victoria, BC, for the last forty years with my husband. I am blessed with a son and daughter, and one grandson. My adopted family gave me caring parents and four lovable brothers and sisters.

Mudgy also gave me a gift of siblings. I am thankful to have met two brothers and four sisters. I am fortunate to share a close bond with my birth sister Barb, who lives in Sechelt, BC. Several years ago, Barb and I travelled to Daylu to see the birthplace of our biological mother and aunt. The significance of two sisters returning to Daylu close to eighty-five years after another two sisters were forced to leave was not lost on us.

However, that is another story to tell.

# Acknowledgements

I WISH to thank the team at Heritage House Publishing. Special thanks to editor Lara Kordic who believed in the value and heart embedded within *Aggie & Mudgy*. Cheers to illustrator Alyssa Koski for the colourful book cover and chapter illustrations.

To friends who agreed to be early readers of the manuscript, Kate, you have a shrewd and artistic eye and always have excellent suggestions. Romola, thank you for reading and saying yes!

Thank you to Monique Gray Smith, who kindly offered feedback on the manuscript and gently suggested it was ready for a nudge into the universe.

To Catherine Lang, author and friend. Your critiques and valuable comments helped navigate the manuscript toward a heartfelt final draft. You are a rock star.

Thank you to my families, my adoptive parents, Bill and Lillian, I know you are both cheering from the cosmos. My adoptive sisters and brothers, you are all champions.

My birth siblings and extended Kaska Dena families, it has been a pleasure getting to know you better over the years. To my sister Barb, thanks for reading *Aggie & Mudgy* and giving me constructive feedback. This is our story!

To my birth mother Mudgy, and Aunty Aggie, we owe a depth of gratitude to both of you. You are survivors and your voices are no longer silent. *Mahsi Cho.*

To my children, Geoff and Tracey, you two are inspiring and I am blessed for all you are and do. To their spouses, Jen and Sam, your kind natures are always a welcome source of cheer. To my two wee grandsons—William and Jacob—thank you for giving us joy and laughter. Finally, this book wouldn't exist without my husband and first reader, Trevor. Your support continues to amaze and delight me.

Final appreciation to all of our ancestors who led the way for future generations to speak, dance, create, and indeed disturb the universe.

# Suggested Reading

City of Vancouver: *Vancouver. First Peoples: A Guide for Newcomers*. vancouver. ca/files/cov/first-peoples-a-guide-for-newcomers.pdf, 2014.

Crey, Ernie, and Suzanne Fournier. *Stolen From Our Embrace*. Vancouver: Douglas & McIntyre, 1998.

Fiske, Jo-Anne. Gender and the Paradox of Residential Education in Carrier Society. Women of the First Nations of Canada: National Symposium. 131–45, 1989.

Fiske, Jo-Anne. And Then We Prayed Again: Carrier Women, Colonialism and Mission Schools. Masters' Thesis. Department of Anthropology and Sociology: University of British Columbia. 1981.

Gray Smith, Monique. *Speaking Our Truth: A Journey of Reconciliation*. Victoria: Orca Book Publishers, 2017.

Johnston, Patrick. *Native Children and the Child Welfare System*. Toronto: James Lorimer and the Canadian Council on Social Development, 1983.

Kaska Language Website. Kaska Language Lessons: Liard Dialect. Pat Moore and Mida Donnessey eds. First Nations Languages 100K, University of British Columbia. kaska.arts.ubc.ca, 2003.

Milloy, John S. *A National Crime: The Canadian Government and the Residential School System—1979 to 1986*. Winnipeg: The University of Manitoba Press, 1999.

Moran, Bridget. *Stoney Creek Woman: The Story of Mary John*. Vancouver: Arsenal Pulp Press Book Publishers Ltd., 1988.

Newman, Carey, and Kirstie Hudson. *Picking up the Pieces*. Victoria: Orca Book Publishers, 2019.

Olsen, Sylvia. *No Time to Say Goodbye: Children's Stories of Kuper Island Residential School*. Winlaw, BC: Sono Nis Press, 2001.

Sinclair, Raven. "Identity Lost and Found: Lessons from the Sixties Scoop." *First Peoples Child & Family Review* 3, no.1, 65–82, 2007.

# Bibliography

Archer, Laurel. *Northern British Columbia Canoe Trips: Volume One*. Victoria: Rocky Mountain Books, 2008.

Demerjian, Bonnie. *Images of America: Wrangell*. Charleston: Arcadia Publishing, 2011.

Duncan, Kate C. *Northern Athapaskan Art: A Beadwork Tradition*. Seattle: University of Washington Press, 1989.

Halpin, Marjorie M., and Seguin, Margaret. "Tsimshian Peoples: Southern Tsimshian, Coast Tsimshian, Nishga, and Gitksan," in *Handbook of North American Indians*, William C. Sturtevant, general editor. Washington, DC: Smithsonian Institution, 267–83, 1978.

Holy Family Mission. Roman Catholic Church Baptismal Records of Kaska Dene Families. Lower Post, BC. 1984.

Honigmann, John J. *Culture and Ethos of Kaska Society*. London: Yale University Press, 1949.

Kaska Dena Council. Kaska Dena Council Home Page. kaskadenacouncil. com (accessed September 10, 2016).

Kaska Dena Heritage Trails Project: Vol. 2. Management Plan for the Southern Davie Trail with Historical Background. November 19, 2000. mackenziemuseum.ca/wordpress/wp-content/uploads/Gunderson-2000-Kaska-Davie-Trail-Report.pdf.

Kerr, Donald, and Deryck W. Holdsworth (eds.). *Historical Atlas of Canada: Addressing the Twentieth Century, 1891-1961*. Toronto: University of Toronto Press, 1990.

Kluckner, Michael. *Vanishing British Columbia*. Vancouver: UBC Press, 2005.

Large, R. Geddes. *The Skeena: River of Destiny*. Surrey, BC: Heritage House Publishing, 1996.

Lutz, John. *Makuk: A New History of Aboriginal-White Relations*. Vancouver: UBC Press, 2008.

Nadleh Whut'en First Nation. Our People: Lejac Residential School. nadleh. ca/our-people/our-history (accessed October 12, 2014).

Prince Rupert City and Regional Archives. princerupertarchives.ca (accessed October 12, 2014).

Regional District of Kitimat-Stikine. Telegraph Creek Townsite. rdks.bc.ca/content/telegraph-creek-townsite (accessed February 3, 2015).

Stolz, Agnes. *Agnes, The Loyal Matriarch*. Self-published personal memoir, 1994.

Super, Natural British Columbia, Canada. Burns Lake—Culture and History. hellobc.com/burns-lake/culture-history.aspx (accessed October 10, 2014).

Teit, James A. "1917 Kaska Tales." *Journal of American Folklore* 30 (118): 427-73.

Truth and Reconciliation Commission of Canada. They Came for the Children: Canada, Aboriginal Peoples, and Residential Schools. Truth and Reconciliation Commission of Canada Report, 2012.

Turner, Robert D. *Sternwheelers and Steam Tugs*. Victoria: Sono Nis Press, 1984.

Vancouver Historical Society Project. *The Story of Vancouver: Vancouver Before It Was*. vancouver-historical-society.ca (accessed November 13, 2014).

# About
## the Author

WENDY PROVERBS is an emerging Indigenous author of Kaska Dena descent. She holds a BA and MA in anthropology from the University of Victoria. Like thousands of Indigenous people across Canada, as an infant she was caught in the sweeping scoop of Indigenous children taken from their birth families and was only reunited with biological family members as a young adult. She has acted as a community liaison with Indigenous communities and strives to help younger generations, both Indigenous and non-Indigenous, learn more about their past.